CHINESE
ASTROLOGY

Inspiring | Educating | Creating | Entertaining

Brimming with creative inspiration, how-to projects, and useful information to enrich your everyday life, quarto.com is a favorite destination for those pursuing their interests and passions.

First published in 2022 by Wellfleet Press,
an imprint of The Quarto Group,
142 West 36th Street, 4th Floor,
New York, NY 10018, USA
T (212) 779-4972 F (212) 779-6058
www.Quarto.com

Wellfleet titles are also available at discount for retail, wholesale, promotional, and bulk purchase. For details, contact the Special Sales Manager by email at specialsales@quarto.com or by mail at The Quarto Group, Attn: Special Sales Manager, 100 Cummings Center Suite, 265D, Beverly, MA 01915 USA.

10 9 8 7 6 5 4 3 2 1

Library of Congress Control Number: 2022934347

ISBN: 978-1-57715-327-6

Publisher: Rage Kindelsperger
Creative Director: Laura Drew
Managing Editor: Cara Donaldson
Cover and Interior Design: Ashley Prine/Tandem Books
Editor: Elizabeth You

Printed in China

This book provides general information on various widely known and widely accepted practices that tend to evoke feelings of strength and confidence. However, it should not be relied upon as recommending or promoting any specific diagnosis or method of treatment for a particular condition, and it is not intended as a substitute for medical advice or for direct diagnosis and treatment of a medical condition by a qualified physician. Readers who have questions about a particular condition, possible treatments for that condition, or possible reactions from the condition or its treatment should consult a physician or other qualified healthcare professional.

The Quarto Group denounces any and all forms of hate, discrimination, and oppression and does not condone the use of its products in any practices aimed at harming or demeaning any group or individual.

IN FOCUS

CHINESE ASTROLOGY

ᐸYour Personal Guideᐳ

SASHA FENTON

WELLFLEET
P R E S S

CONTENTS

INTRODUCTION

Like Western astrology, Chinese astrology started as a way of using the positions of the stars to predict future events, but over time, it came to incorporate Confucianism, myths, legends, and numerology. While the basics of Chinese astrology are easy to grasp, the subject becomes increasingly intricate the more you learn, until it reaches mind-bending levels of complexity.

This introductory book covers the basics and is divided into two parts. Chinese astrology years are based on the lunar calendar, which begins with the new moon sometime between January 21 and February 20. The first, and by far the largest, part covers the basics of the character of each of the animal year signs, along with the way the five zodiac elements (wood, fire, earth, metal, water) modify their nature. This is followed by a forecasting section that shows how each sign will fare over time.

In the second section, I go into a little more depth and cover the month signs, the seasons, the day signs, and the hour signs. I end the book by showing you how the Four Pillars of Destiny Chinese horoscope chart works, including examples of what each pillar means.

Though I am not an expert on Chinese astrology, I have experience with the subject and have used a number of primary sources for research. If you are keen to understand the basics of this subject, this book is a good starting point. Readers can also refer to the enclosed poster for a brief description of each of the twelve signs.

* * *

For much of its long history, China was isolated from other cultures. The Chinese people developed their own astrological systems and interpretations independently of Middle Eastern or Western concepts. Chinese astrology dates to the Zhou dynasty (1046–256 BC), and it was popular during the Han dynasty, which ruled from the second century BC to the second century AD. This was when the notions of the polarities of yin and yang emerged, along with the five elements and traditional Chinese medicine.

Chinese culture sometimes emphasizes different priorities than Western culture. Family success and taking care of elders are considered important, and while of course people marry for love, compatibility between partners and getting along with each other's family are highly prioritized. So, while I have tried to cover all aspects including love and family life, you will notice glimpses of the astrological system's emphasis on financial and social status. Also, money is commonly associated with fortune, so divination about finances is essentially divination about good and bad luck.

Enclosed Chinese Astrology Wall Chart

Included in this book is a Chinese astrology wall chart that serves as a quick and handy reference guide.

PART I

THE YEAR SIGNS AND THE ELEMENTS

1

THE YEAR SIGNS

nlike the Western zodiac, which is made up of animals, people, and one inanimate object (the Scales), the signs in the Chinese zodiac are all animals, apart from the Dragon, which is a mythical beast. Each animal represents a year in a twelve-year cycle. Their usual order is:

- Rat
- Ox
- Tiger
- Rabbit
- Dragon
- Snake
- Horse
- Goat
- Monkey
- Rooster
- Dog
- Pig

An Ancient Legend

There is a rather lovely legend associated with the order in which the animal signs are listed. Long ago, the ruler of the universe (some say the Jade Emperor or Buddha) decided that all the animals of service to humans should run a race to establish the zodiac signs. The Rat received his invitation to attend and told the other animals; however, his friend the Cat was worried that he might oversleep, so he made the Rat promise to wake him in plenty of time. This was a task that the Rat neglected to do, so the Cat never made it to the starting line, and this is why cats loathe rodents to this day. On the morning of the race, eleven animals lined up, ready to start, knowing the first one to reach the feet of the Supreme Being would have the honor of becoming the first sign of the zodiac. The Supreme Being noticed that one animal was absent, so he sent his advisor down to the earth to find an extra contestant to fill the gap. The first animal the advisor encountered was a small, fat pig, so he seized the animal and brought it to the starting line without further ado.

Finally, all was ready, and at a signal, they set off. The faster creatures, the Dragon, Horse, and Tiger, set the pace, but they soon became tired and fell behind. The tenacity of the Ox proved to be the winning trait, so he shouldered the Tiger aside and looked as though he was going to be the victor. But just as the Ox was about to reach the finish line, the cunning Rat, who had concealed himself in the Ox's tail, ran the length of the Ox's back and jumped off the end of his nose.

The Supreme Being was very impressed by the Rat's ingenuity but was still not sure he had won the race fairly. The Rat produced a flute and began to play

and dance to clinch the matter, which amused the Almighty and persuaded him to award the Rat the honor anyway. By the time the Rat had finished his antics, the fat little Pig had finally shuffled up to the last position. And that is how the order of the zodiac signs was established.

Of course, China is a big place with a very long history, and as we saw in the introduction, Chinese astrology is found all over the East, so it isn't surprising there are discrepancies in names. The table below shows the most commonly used Western names, followed by their Chinese names, and then some common variations that you may come across.

Modern Western Names	Chinese Names	Variations
Rat	shu	Mouse
Ox	niu	Bull, Buffalo, Water Buffalo, Cow
Tiger	hu	
Rabbit	tu	Hare, Cat (in Vietnam)
Dragon	long	Snail (in Kazakhstan)
Snake	she	Serpent
Horse	ma	Antelope
Goat	yang	Sheep, Ram, Lamb
Monkey	hou	Ape
Rooster	ji	Cockerel, Cock, Fowl, Bird, Chicken, Hen
Dog	gou	Wolf
Pig	zhu	Boar, Wild Boar (in Japan)

The Lunar Year

The best way to begin understanding Chinese astrology is to look up your year sign below. The list gives dates for Chinese years and each year's polarity, element, and animal sign.

Some Chinese astrologers dispense with the lunar year and its "floating" dates and settle instead on a solar year that starts on February 4. However, in this book, I have stuck to tradition and provided the lunar year dates.

Year	Starts	Polarity	Element	Animal
1930	Jan 29	Yang	Metal	Horse
1931	Feb 17	Yin	Metal	Goat
1932	Feb 6	Yang	Water	Monkey
1933	Jan 25	Yin	Water	Rooster
1934	Feb 14	Yang	Wood	Dog
1935	Feb 3	Yin	Wood	Pig
1936	Jan 24	Yang	Fire	Rat
1937	Feb 11	Yin	Fire	Ox
1938	Jan 31	Yang	Earth	Tiger
1939	Feb 19	Yin	Earth	Rabbit
1940	Feb 8	Yang	Metal	Dragon
1941	Jan 27	Yin	Metal	Snake

Year	Starts	Polarity	Element	Animal
1942	Feb 15	Yang	Water	Horse
1943	Feb 4	Yin	Water	Goat
1944	Jan 25	Yang	Wood	Monkey
1945	Feb 12	Yin	Wood	Rooster
1946	Feb 2	Yang	Fire	Dog
1947	Jan 22	Yin	Fire	Pig
1948	Feb 10	Yang	Earth	Rat
1949	Jan 29	Yin	Earth	Ox
1950	Feb 16	Yang	Metal	Tiger
1951	Feb 6	Yin	Metal	Rabbit
1952	Jan 26	Yang	Water	Dragon
1953	Feb 14	Yin	Water	Snake
1954	Feb 3	Yang	Wood	Horse
1955	Jan 24	Yin	Wood	Goat
1956	Feb 11	Yang	Fire	Monkey
1957	Jan 30	Yin	Fire	Rooster
1958	Feb 18	Yang	Earth	Dog
1959	Feb 7	Yin	Earth	Pig
1960	Jan 28	Yang	Metal	Rat
1961	Feb 15	Yin	Metal	Ox

Year	Starts	Polarity	Element	Animal
1962	Feb 5	Yang	Water	Tiger
1963	Jan 25	Yin	Water	Rabbit
1964	Feb 13	Yang	Wood	Dragon
1965	Feb 1	Yin	Wood	Snake
1966	Jan 21	Yang	Fire	Horse
1967	Feb 9	Yin	Fire	Goat
1968	Jan 29	Yang	Earth	Monkey
1969	Feb 16	Yin	Earth	Rooster
1970	Feb 6	Yang	Metal	Dog
1971	Jan 26	Yin	Metal	Pig
1972	Feb 15	Yang	Water	Rat
1973	Feb 3	Yin	Water	Ox
1974	Jan 24	Yang	Wood	Tiger
1975	Feb 11	Yin	Wood	Rabbit
1976	Jan 31	Yang	Fire	Dragon
1977	Feb 18	Yin	Fire	Snake

Year	Starts	Polarity	Element	Animal
1978	Feb 7	Yang	Earth	Horse
1979	Jan 28	Yin	Earth	Goat
1980	Feb 16	Yang	Metal	Monkey
1981	Feb 5	Yin	Metal	Rooster
1982	Jan 25	Yang	Water	Dog
1983	Feb 13	Yin	Water	Pig
1984	Feb 2	Yang	Wood	Rat
1985	Feb 20	Yin	Wood	Ox
1986	Feb 9	Yang	Fire	Tiger
1987	Jan 29	Yin	Fire	Rabbit
1988	Feb 17	Yang	Earth	Dragon
1989	Feb 6	Yin	Earth	Snake
1990	Jan 26	Yang	Metal	Horse
1991	Feb 14	Yin	Metal	Goat
1992	Feb 3	Yang	Water	Monkey
1993	Jan 22	Yin	Water	Rooster

Year	Starts	Polarity	Element	Animal
1994	Feb 10	Yang	Wood	Dog
1995	Jan 31	Yin	Wood	Pig
1996	Feb 19	Yang	Fire	Rat
1997	Feb 7	Yin	Fire	Ox
1998	Jan 28	Yang	Earth	Tiger
1999	Jan 16	Yin	Earth	Rabbit
2000	Feb 5	Yang	Metal	Dragon
2001	Jan 24	Yin	Metal	Snake
2002	Feb 12	Yang	Water	Horse
2003	Feb 1	Yin	Water	Goat
2004	Jan 22	Yang	Wood	Monkey
2005	Feb 9	Yin	Wood	Rooster
2006	Jan 29	Yang	Fire	Dog
2007	Feb 18	Yin	Fire	Pig
2008	Feb 7	Yang	Earth	Rat
2009	Jan 26	Yin	Earth	Ox
2010	Feb 14	Yang	Metal	Tiger

Year	Starts	Polarity	Element	Animal
2011	Feb 3	Yin	Metal	Rabbit
2012	Jan 23	Yang	Water	Dragon
2013	Feb 10	Yin	Water	Snake
2014	Jan 30	Yang	Wood	Horse
2015	Jan 20	Yin	Wood	Goat
2016	Feb 8	Yang	Fire	Monkey
2017	Jan 28	Yin	Fire	Rooster
2018	Feb 15	Yang	Earth	Dog
2019	Feb 4	Yin	Earth	Pig
2020	Jan 24	Yang	Metal	Rat
2021	Feb 12	Yin	Metal	Ox
2022	Feb 1	Yang	Water	Tiger
2023	Jan 23	Yin	Water	Rabbit
2024	Feb 10	Yang	Wood	Dragon
2025	Jan 29	Yin	Wood	Snake
2026	Feb 17	Yang	Fire	Horse
2027	Feb 6	Yin	Fire	Goat
2028	Jan 26	Yang	Earth	Monkey
2029	Feb 13	Yin	Earth	Rooster
2030	Feb 3	Yang	Metal	Dog

✻ ✻ ✻

(2)

THE
ELEMENTS

The Nature of the Elements

Along with the animal signs, the five elements of wood, fire, earth, metal, and water have their own nature and energies, which are described below.

The Elements

Wood   Fire   Earth   Metal   Water

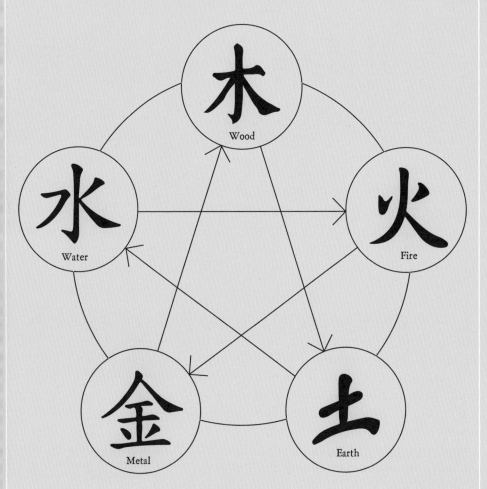

The Element of Wood

- The ancient archetype is the wise advisor to the emperor, and the element is associated with agriculture.
- Planetary link: Jupiter.

CONNECTIONS

Wood is associated with springtime, birth, and anything that needs to grow.

WOOD PEOPLE

These are the intellectuals, teachers, honest and decent people who are not particularly streetwise. Wood people are quiet, studious, serious, and have a dry sense of humor. This element rules those who are wise in the ways of agriculture and farming.

Idealistic, compassionate, creative, and imaginative, wood people have a youthful attitude. With the right circumstances and with plenty of support, they can do well at work and have a good life. They like to make plans and start projects, but they don't have the patience to carry them through to the end. They can be irritable and disorganized, but they do well with a supportive partner and helpful colleagues. Like trees, they are hard to uproot, preferring to stay in one place or one situation. However, if they have to make major changes and even leave their country of birth, they do so without looking back.

The downside is that they are quick to react and to take offense, impatient, impulsive, rash, and they can be territorial. They are advised to control their impulsive nature and their temper.

WOOD CAREERS

Wood people enjoy music, so many can be found in that industry. As this element is a living plant, any job related to wood or plants would be perfect, such as growing and cooking vegetables and fruit or making herb tea. This talent also lends itself to working with traditional Chinese therapies and medicines, as well as careers in the fields of education, publishing, clothing, and fashion.

WOOD HEALTH

Wood people can overwork and suffer from tension as a result, with headaches and other stress-related problems. Their systems are sensitive, and they can suffer from allergies, intolerances, and auto-immune issues. Their livers, gallbladders, eyes, and tendons may be weak, and women may suffer from menstrual problems.

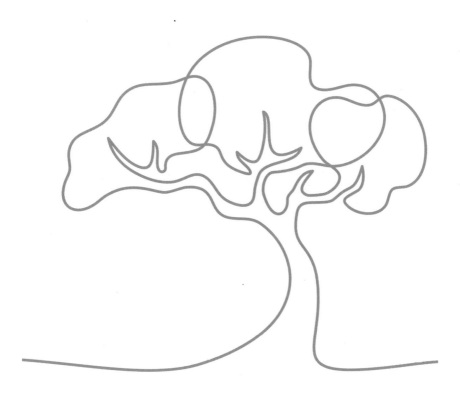

The Element of Fire

• The ancient archetype is that of the emperor's war leader, general, or admiral, always ready to fight for a good cause.
• Planetary link: Mars.

CONNECTIONS

This element is associated with summer; as far as agriculture is concerned, this is the most productive phase, when everyone helps with the farming and the harvest. Depending on where one lives, the season varies from warm to hot, sometimes too hot for comfort.

FIRE PEOPLE

Fire people are productive and hardworking, warm, enthusiastic, optimistic, and passionate about everything they do. They may take up causes, get involved in politics or social work, and do all they can to help others. These people make good counselors and therapists, and their advice is worth taking. They are attractive, charming, and popular, passionate and loving. They like to stay close to their parents, even when they have families of their own.

The downside is that they can be overly optimistic and unrealistic; they may exaggerate and be too flamboyant. They may jump into situations without appraising them sufficiently first. Fire people don't compromise, and they can be defensive and argumentative.

FIRE CAREERS

Suitable jobs include anything to do with fire, such as the fuel and energy industry, and even the manufacture of products such as firearms or cooking equipment. This strength also lends itself to engineering, cooking, and working in restaurants. Other suitable options include advertising, the airline industry, and working with products that enhance our appearance, such as dress design and tailoring, cosmetics, and hairdressing.

FIRE HEALTH

These choleric folk may suffer from high blood pressure, leading to heart problems and strokes. Their eyes may need attention. They may have trouble with the small intestine, tongue, and blood circulation. Not surprisingly, fire people need properly cooked meals and don't do well with salads and raw vegetables.

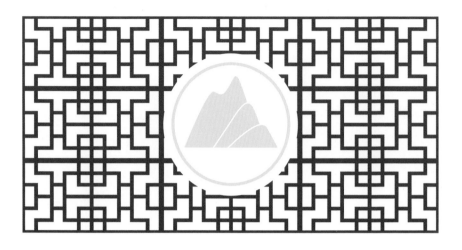

The Element of Earth

- The ancient connection is to the court, China, and possibly the emperor himself.
- Planetary link: Saturn.

CONNECTIONS

This element represents the center and the heart of everything. In days gone by, earth represented the emperor and the kingdom of China. Therefore, this element rules land, which is solid, unchanging, and as difficult to move as a mountain. It connects with the ideas of the harvest, grain stores, and cattle, and thus wealth.

EARTH PEOPLE

Earth people are hard workers who can be relied upon to do a job thoroughly. They may not show this trait when young, but they grow up to be dutiful, dependable, caring, and rational people who can reach the very top of whatever job they take on. They are highly intelligent, well-read, capable, and they never stop learning. Earth folk value their friends and keep them for years. They don't like change and will keep to the same routine for as long as possible.

They may overthink things and become dissatisfied and depressed if life doesn't go their way. At worst, they lack passion and positivity, and they can become downhearted or angry. They can go to extremes, either going to a lot of trouble explaining their interests or losing patience and energy and not wanting to give any kind of explanation to anybody.

EARTH CAREERS

Traditionally, this element is associated with agriculture, mining, construction, tiling, stonework, masonry, and security in the form of locks and alarms, along with insurance, finance for homes, and accountancy. This element was also linked to running an estate, but today this translates into running a business, especially where computers and finance are concerned. This sign relates to great success in business or the field of sports or any other competitive sphere. Jobs can also be found in the funeral and undertaking world for this element.

HEALTH

Earth people may experience problems with the bowels and bladder, but also with breathing, weak muscles, and possibly heart trouble. The spleen may be weak, and as this organ functions best in warm weather and a dry atmosphere, it is good for Earth people to live in warm climates. They may have problems with the mouth or the stomach.

The Element of Metal

• The ancient link is to the keeper of the emperor's art galleries, the opera, and the creation of beauty in the form of pottery and crafts.
• Planetary link: Venus.

CONNECTIONS

This element is associated with autumn, so it's tied to clearing clutter, cleaning things out, and, in particular, cleaning and mending tools and farming implements in preparation for winter. It is time to stock the cupboards, sell produce, and pay debts.

The Metal element links to the arts, the Chinese opera, the finer things in life, celebrity, beautiful clothes, music, color, gourmet food, fine dining, fame, and amusements such as gambling and games such as mahjong and similar enjoyable pastimes.

METAL PEOPLE

These people are strong personalities and high flyers with legal minds, so they do well in business, law, politics, and any arena where they can reach for the top. They are fair, decisive, single-minded, and firm, ambitious, competitive, and demanding, but also humanitarian and keen to make the world a better place. They are highly strung and intense, but most of all, they are unafraid of people or problems and determined to overcome everything. They can be very amusing and good company, but they are probably better as friends than in romantic relationships because they can't compromise.

The downside is that they can be selfish, inflexible, and obstinate, with little compassion, focus, and intention of doing anything useful.

METAL CAREERS

Politics is an ideal arena for these idealistic people as are engineering and making steel and metals. Other possible careers include producing and selling cutlery, surgical instruments, tools, or weapons of all kinds. Surgery is another option. These people might also be involved in manufacturing, marketing, and fixing motor vehicles. Other possible careers include the world of jewelry, including gold, silver, and decorative metalwork; the legal world, government and the police, banking, finance, and the stock market. Metal people may be led into the worlds of fashion and beauty, games and toys, the travel trade, or the entertainment industry.

HEALTH

The bones and connections between them may cause problems for Metal people, so there might be slipped discs or issues with the hips and knees, especially in old age. Deafness is a possibility, as are breathing difficulties or trouble with the large intestine, leading to constipation and irritable bowel syndrome. They may also have problems with the nose and skin. Worry and tension cause many of their problems.

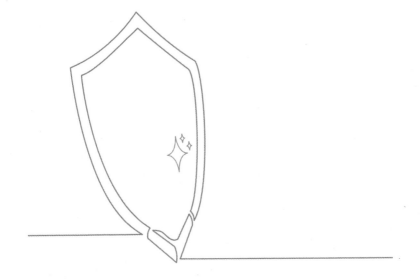

The Element of Water

• The ancient association is that of the emperor's treasurer, traders, travelers, news, and the construction industry.

• Planetary link: Mercury.

CONNECTIONS

Water is tied to the depth of winter, when the landscape is covered in frost and snow and looks beautiful, but everything is quiet. This is a time of rest, recovery, and mystery.

This element was once linked to the treasures of the court, and to finance and banking. It was mainly connected to commerce and communications via the rivers and canals that were China's trade routes, along with coastal shipping and travels to other lands. It was particularly associated with communications, information, commerce, exploration, exploitation for trade, and probably spying for the emperor; also civil engineering, construction, engineering as a whole, and thus on to mathematics and astrology.

WATER PEOPLE

The best characteristics of these lovely people are wisdom, intelligence, a philosophical attitude, and adaptability. They are highly intelligent, witty, and eloquent, and they make great negotiators and strategists who encourage others to follow them. Artistic and creative, with a love of the good things in life, these people are the gentlest of all the elemental types. They are compassionate and love to help and encourage others, but they hate it when others take advantage of their good nature. They must learn to set boundaries to avoid living with partners who may not respect them and they need to learn to say no when it is necessary. They need freedom and to avoid being pushed around or bullied.

Some people look down on Water folk and consider them weak or ideal victims for their abuse. Still, Water subjects often become more successful, better off, more respected, and far more loved than those who abuse them.

Water people are extremely sensitive, so they react badly to sharp-tongued people or those who disrespect them. Their intuition may be so strong they almost seem psychic, so they can't be tricked, and they sum others up very quickly. They can be fearful, unstable, fickle, and very nervous, and if very upset, they even lose their ability to make money.

WATER CAREERS

Water people have several strings to their bows, one being travel and transport, such as taxi driving, working in the travel trade, or the import and export industry where they move goods around. Business is a natural arena for Water people, as is anything creative or anything that interests or entertains the public. They can do well as writers. They are quick to spot opportunities, and they are likely to be far more successful than their gentle demeanor suggests. Some are great counselors and therapists, while others work in the legal arena. They may work in the bottled water industry, fishing, or clearing and dredging lakes and rivers. They may also work with swimming pools, spas, and the wellness industry, or complementary therapies, medicine, and even dentistry. This element also rules cleaning, laundry, and dry cleaning.

HEALTH

Water retention might be a problem, but so could the renal system, because the prevailing emotion is fear, which affects the kidneys badly. The bladder is so sensitive that it can lead to incontinence with age, along with hearing problems and arthritis.

❋ ❋ ❋

3

THE ANIMAL
YEAR SIGNS

This chapter shows the nature and characteristics of each sign based on lunar year.

The Year Sign

This represents our outer manner and the first impression we give to others. It also describes the surroundings and general lifestyle that we find ourselves living in, especially during the early years of our lives.

The Rat: 1936, 1948, 1960, 1972, 1984, 1996, 2008, 2020	**The Ox:** 1937, 1949, 1961, 1973, 1985, 1997, 2009, 2021	**The Tiger:** 1938, 1950, 1962, 1974, 1986, 1998, 2010, 2022	**The Rabbit:** 1939, 1951, 1963, 1975, 1987, 1999, 2011, 2023
The Dragon: 1940, 1952, 1964, 1976, 1988, 2000, 2012, 2024	**The Snake:** 1941, 1953, 1965, 1977, 1989, 2001, 2013, 2025	**The Horse:** 1930, 1942, 1954, 1966, 1978, 1990, 2002, 2014, 2026	**The Goat:** 1931, 1943, 1955, 1967, 1979, 1991, 2003, 2015, 2027
The Monkey: 1932, 1944, 1956, 1968, 1980, 1992, 2004, 2016, 2028	**The Rooster:** 1933, 1945, 1957, 1969, 1981, 1993, 2005, 2017, 2029	**The Dog:** 1934, 1946, 1958, 1970, 1982, 1994, 2006, 2018, 2030	**The Pig:** 1935, 1947, 1959, 1971, 1983, 1995, 2007, 2019

The Nature of the Rat

Years: 1936, 1948, 1960, 1972, 1984, 1996, 2008, 2020

Polarity: Yang

Key attribute: A survivor

Worst attributes: Crafty, calculating

Rats symbolize charm, intelligence, good business sense, intuition, enterprise, and money-making ability—although these people don't always manage to hang on to the money they make. People born under this sign are intelligent, shrewd, assertive, and well able to look after their interests. They have pleasant personalities and are sociable, popular, tasteful, and charming, and they have a great sense of humor. They are good communicators, and some of them are idealistic. They are talented, adaptable, open-minded, and intellectual, and for the most part, honest and dependable.

Their primary attribute is their ability to find ways around difficult situations, thus ensuring their survival during times of turmoil. They can even take up jobs or ways of life that are entirely different from what they are used to if the need arises, and they welcome a change of scene and a new adventure. Rats are ambitious and resourceful—after all, if we consider the legend of the race, it was the Rat that won, despite being the smallest animal; Rats can find ways of making things work, even when others cannot. They like a change of environment, so they move house fairly often and take up new interests whenever boredom sets in.

Rats dress well, try to keep their weight within limits, and look after their skin and hair. They have a youthful outlook, and they get on well with young people. Their childhood may not have been a bed of roses, and they can lose out to brothers and sisters whom their parents prefer.

On a negative note, they can gossip and bad-mouth others, and they can be critical, selfish, greedy, and unwilling to compromise. Some are wasteful and others are hoarders.

Rat Love and Friendship

Rats are extremely devoted to those they love, sometimes obsessively so. If a Rat wants someone who isn't accessible or doesn't feel the same way about them, they may find it hard to accept, so they may make themselves and everyone around them miserable. Rats are more vulnerable than they look, and when young, they let partners know too much about the things that hurt them, which allows their lovers to take advantage of them. Eventually, Rats do make good relationships, and they are generous to and supportive of their partners. They can be sexy, but they are more interested in their family and work than running around looking for sexual outlets.

- Compatible for love with the Ox, the Monkey, or the Dragon.
- Friendship or love with the Tiger, the Snake, the Pig, and with other Rats.
- Friendship with the Dog.
- Signs that have no particular effect one way or another are the Rabbit, the Horse, the Goat, and the Rooster.

Rat Careers

The Rat's complex personality can make a career out of any opportunity that presents itself, and they work hard and are reliable. They are not as confident as they seem, though, so they may be prone to worry and can't stand criticism or mockery. They work hard to succeed even when the odds are against them. They have academic minds, so they do well in scientific subjects, or as historians, journalists, or broadcasters.

Rat Health

The kidneys, bladder, prostate, and urethra are likely to cause problems for the Rat. The Rat needs to drink plenty of water and keep their salt intake to a minimum. Rats can overindulge in food or alcohol, both of which may cause problems later in life. Another problem is they tend to be high strung and not handle stress well, leading to inflammation of nerves around the head or spine, as well as toothaches. Rats benefit from any stress-reducing activity.

Rat Luck

Rats are believed to have a better life if born at night or during the summer months. Rats born in the daytime or the winter have less self-confidence and are less enterprising and less successful, but they have better luck in matters of love.

The Rat Elements

 ### THE WOOD RAT (1984)

Wood endows even more intelligence to the clever Rat, so these are true academics whose insight and intuition make them able to spot trends. These Rats need emotional security and money put by for a rainy day.

 ### THE FIRE RAT (1936, 1996)

Fire endows courage, assertiveness, and a sharp tongue, but these Rats are idealistic and willing to fight for the underdog. They are the most highly sexed of the Rats, and they are happy if that side of things works for them; otherwise, they destroy the relationship.

 ### THE EARTH RAT (1948, 2008)

These Rats work hard because they need security and money, maybe to compensate for early deprivation. They may marry young, possibly to escape a difficult family situation, and this may turn out to be a mistake, but they learn from their blunders.

 ### THE METAL RAT (1960, 2020)

These Rats work their way through difficulties with dogged determination. Their willpower, perfectionism, and natural athleticism help them succeed at sports. While their charm is endearing, their relationships can be filled with turmoil and jealousy.

 ### THE WATER RAT (1972)

These intellectuals achieve much and inspire respect, are diplomatic, and they find ways through problems without offending others. They are cool, critical, and appear unemotional because they keep their feelings hidden. These Rats love to travel.

The Nature of the Ox

Years: 1937, 1949, 1961, 1973, 1985, 1997, 2009, 2021

Polarity: Yin

Key attribute: Tenacity

Worst attributes: Obstinacy, greed

Ox people are practical, sensible, and capable, and they do exceptionally well in life once they find their métier. Many of them seem to be lucky when it comes to inheriting money, property, or businesses. They are strong, healthy, and robust, so they can live long and productive lives if they care for themselves. Many are home-loving and true family people, although some have extremely itchy feet and don't take well to the restrictions of family life. All Oxen love a comfortable home, good food, and expensive holidays. These people have excellent taste and style, some are artistic or musical, and many are excellent dancers. They love their surroundings to be attractive, and they can't stand living in a mess. They love to travel, and they are good company when on holiday, so they are happy to have a group of people around them. These people are well turned out, pleasant, friendly, good-humored, and classy.

Oxen are steady workers who don't give up easily, so they make a success of their careers, and they provide well for their families. Many grow up in families where religion or some set of rules makes life trying, but whatever the circumstances, they eventually make their own choices and their own way in life.

These people need time alone to recharge their batteries and enjoy their hobbies in peace. Pleasant as they are, their faults are obstinacy, stinginess, greed, and a nasty tongue when they want to hurt others. Some are positively cold-hearted and unromantic, sexual but unloving; however, Oxen do what they can for their children and other relatives.

Ox Love and Friendship

Oxen marry while they are young, and they stay with their lover for good unless the partner leaves. Females are excellent housewives who are amazingly good at the traditional roles, and they make dutiful and reliable wives. Males can be the dedicated, capable, home-loving husbands many women want, but some are complainers, though they will help with the housework. Male Oxen have practical skills, such as do-it-yourself fixes, gardening, and cooking. There are also restless types of male Oxen who are womanizers. Although they love their children, Oxen won't sacrifice much for them. They can even put their children into boarding schools if their careers involve traveling or being unavailable to the family. They are sexy, sometimes too much so.

- Compatible for love with the Rat, the Snake, and the Rooster.
- Friendship only with the Dragon, the Rabbit, the Monkey, and the Pig.
- Incompatible with the Tiger, the Horse, the Dog, and the Goat.
- A sign that has no particular effect one way or another is the Ox.

Ox Careers

Oxen start out pursuing practical professions, such as engineering, construction, farming, real estate, police work, education, or catering, but soon move into the higher echelons and become executives. They are often skilled craftspeople who take pride in doing a good job. They are reliable workers, and if they become managers or start their own farms or businesses, they put in the hours and make a success of themselves because they like status and money.

Ox Health

This is a strong sign, and these people can live a long time, but unfortunately, their tendency to eat fatty foods can cause cholesterol to collect in the arteries around their hearts, lower abdomens, and legs. Their digestive systems may become overloaded, and they may have diabetes. They hold anger inside and eventually explode in a bad temper, putting further strain on their hearts, so they need to talk about their problems and relax.

Ox Luck

Oxen make their own luck by working hard—often too hard—but they also take advantage of opportunities when they arise.

The Ox Elements

THE WOOD OX (1985)

These are honest people who have strong ethics, and they are intelligent, capable, and friendly, kindhearted and more considerate than most Oxen. They are forward-thinking, fond of trying new concepts, and are thrifty and careful with money.

THE FIRE OX (1937, 1997)

These individuals may be good at sports or dancing, especially when young. They are charismatic, ambitious, and ruthless when pursuing success, sometimes arrogant and determined to have their own way, but they are also hard workers who are absolutely honest.

THE EARTH OX (1949, 2009)

These people are practical and sensible, sincere, hardworking, and very loyal. They overcome most difficulties through perseverance and tenacity. They are good-natured, reasonable, and they win out in the end. They are faithful to their partners.

THE METAL OX (1961, 2021)

These people are strong-willed, with a desire to do exactly what they want. Metal Oxen are tough, so they don't allow others to push them around. They do well in emergencies and can take charge of any situation that is life-threatening.

THE WATER OX (1973)

These Oxen make wonderful friends and good listeners who don't judge others. They may not get rich, but they make the best of things without complaint. They are good team workers, but their love lives may be disastrous due to their jealousy and suspicion.

The Nature of the Tiger

Years: 1938, 1950, 1962, 1974, 1986, 1998, 2010, 2022

Polarity: Yang

Key attribute: Power

Worst attributes: Bullying, jealousy

These people are warriors who will fend off anybody who tries to attack them. One Chinese legend states that this ferocious beast received one stripe on his forehead for each creature he defeated. Mighty Tigers are humanitarians, so they will stand up for the rights of the underdog.

Tigers have a better childhood than most, probably because they don't put up with anything they don't like, and they don't hesitate to speak up. They are popular with their teachers because their intelligence means they sail through schoolwork, and their size, power, fearlessness, and courage mean they excel at sports, becoming the leaders of the pack whom others most want to be with and to follow.

These fascinating personalities are warm-hearted, honorable, optimistic, and independent, but they are also vain. They are friendly, kind, humorous, and cheerful. However, those who seek to take advantage of their good nature will fail, because Tigers are not easily fooled. The sunny, lighthearted façade conceals a hot temper and a great deal of inner strength. If they find themselves in the middle of a disaster, they rush toward it, rescue others, and become heroes. They like the rewards of leadership and being in executive positions, and they enjoy wealth and status. As they are big spenders, they also need to be well paid. Tigers don't think about the past or worry about the future because they live in the moment, doing what needs to be done right now.

The downside of this sign is that they can be hot-headed, reckless, and rash, suffering from ailments typical of the choleric personality, such as heart attacks or strokes.

Tiger Love and Friendship

On the one hand, this selfish sign may be so interested in pleasing itself that it can't settle for a marriage-type relationship. Tigers don't like being told what they can and can't do. Their charismatic natures ensure that they are unlikely to be short of admirers, which makes them even more unstable. However, some

Tigers do settle into conventional relationships, and their partners and children might feel particularly comforted by the fact that they are under the wing of such powerful and protective partners.

Friends must be as wealthy and successful as the Tiger is, if not more so. Some people are too unnerved by them and frightened of them to want to be their friends, and some avoid working with them because they fear the Tigers will push them around.

- Compatible for love with the Dragon, the Horse, and the Dog.
- Friendship only with the Rat, the Rabbit, the Rooster, and the Pig.
- Incompatible with the Goat, the Ox, the Snake, and the Monkey.
- A sign that has no particular effect one way or another is the Tiger.

Tiger Careers

Tigers need variety in their work, and they need it to feel important or valuable, so they often run their own businesses. They are competent leaders who can inspire loyalty, as long as they don't become bullies. They like design, journalism, broadcasting, and the travel trade. Their physical and mental strength may lead them to become professional sportspeople or go into the police or the armed forces. However, their idealism can also lead them into politics and working for the disadvantaged. They can write well, so they may choose to work in advertising or maybe write adventure stories for a living.

Tiger Health

This is an adventurous sign, so good health depends on getting out and about and not being tied down in a trying or depressing situation. However, their fondness for extreme sports or activities can lead to accidents, so they need a good first-aid kit with them wherever they go! They can overwork and overdo things generally, so they should build in time to relax. Eating fresh fruit and vegetables will help to cleanse their digestive systems.

Tiger Luck

Tigers can bring bad fortune upon themselves if they rush into a relationship before they've brought a previous one to a close.

The Tiger Elements

THE WOOD TIGER (1974)
Wood Tigers want the limelight and have an artistic streak, so they may work in the film industry or something original and unusual. They usually do well and earn good money, but they may never succeed in love relationships.

THE FIRE TIGER (1986)
Fire adds courage, recklessness, and intelligence, so these Tigers may be devious and hurtful. They are extremely knowledgeable, and their charisma fascinates others. Sexy and passionate, they are loyal, but they can be jealous and possessive.

THE EARTH TIGER (1938, 1998)
These Tigers tend to leave home young and soon start to climb the ladder of success. They are excellent, down-to-earth, and practical leaders whose judgment is sound. They are faithful lovers, although possessive and moody.

THE METAL TIGER (1950, 2010)
Metal Tigers are determined and powerful, and they may be egotistic and domineering. Although good fun on a social level, they take too many risks in business. While they can become rich, they can also lose everything. Living with them may be difficult.

THE WATER TIGER (1962, 2022)
These Tigers lead by persuasion and can empathize with others. In addition to ambition and resourcefulness, they see gaps in the market where others cannot. They may make a mess of their lives by starting new relationships while still involved in previous ones.

The Nature of the Rabbit

Years: 1939, 1951, 1963, 1975, 1987, 1999, 2011, 2023

Polarity: Yin

Key attribute: Refinement

Worst attribute: Fussiness

The Rabbit is considered to be the sign of virtue. It represents refinement, high standards, and prudence, and even the Buddha is believed to have taken the form of a Rabbit in one of his previous incarnations. Rabbits are sensitive, well-behaved, and tasteful, but they can be snobs, although not all of them are. They like to look cool and able to do anything, but they are quite nervy and sensitive. They don't mind causing drama, but they get upset if someone else decides to make a fuss. They are considerate, gracious, and sophisticated, so they don't like messy places or situations, and they work hard to ensure they have a lovely home and an attractive place of work.

Rabbits are much more intelligent than they may look, and they work harder than people realize, so given time, they succeed in the career of their choice. Although not necessarily good-looking, they are often interesting and quietly charismatic, so they do well with the opposite sex. They are friendly, decent people, but they can be misunderstood.

Rabbits may be out of step with their parents and siblings, so they go their own way without taking their families' likes and dislikes into consideration. Sometimes this is a matter of survival, because trying to please their relatives could destroy them. They can be fussy, talkative, self-righteous, or hypochondriacs, but most have more common sense than to be so unpleasant. They can be somewhat mysterious, and many are intuitive to the point of seeming psychic.

Rabbits have a reputation for being long-lived, so they need to ensure they have good pension plans to be comfortable in later life.

Rabbit Love and Friendship

Rabbits make excellent friends, and their intelligence and sense of humor make them interesting companions. As lovers, they may attract those who want to take care of them or rule them, so they may choose motherly or fatherly types who will take the strain of daily life off their shoulders. Other Rabbits are hard to please, with an angry nature that bursts out from time to time, making everyone around them highly unsettled and unhappy. They can be sarcastic, hurtful, and difficult, with a habit of pouting and slamming doors. Rabbits desperately need tenderness, understanding, trust, and security within a close relationship and someone who understands them and who can put up with them.

- Compatible for love with the Goat, the Dog, and the Pig.
- Love and friendship with the Horse, the Snake, and the Ox.
- Incompatible with the Dragon, the Rooster, and the Rat.
- Signs that have no particular effect one way or another are the Tiger, the Rabbit, and the Monkey.

Rabbit Careers

Rabbits are brilliant, quick thinking, and completely honest, so they are comfortable working as accountants or in the financial areas of business, banking, and risk analysis. They may become civil servants, dealing with people who need help. If one career doesn't work out for them, they can find another. With their refined nature, it isn't surprising that they are drawn to the world of art, antiques, and other things of beauty. Some may work as jewelers or in the sale of high-end goods to discerning customers. They don't enjoy pressure, so they work best at their own pace. They may work as writers, librarians, artists, or designers. They excel at public relations, so they may become diplomats, lawyers, judges, or court reporters.

Rabbit Health

Rabbits are real squeaky wheels because they are not physically or mentally strong, and stress upsets them badly. Yet, despite this, they have a reputation for being long-lived. Rabbits need a peaceful home life, and they need to avoid too much alcohol and rich foods and even limit such things as olive oil, as this can give them problems with their livers or gallbladders. They aren't physically strong enough for heavy work, as this would damage their weak backs.

Rabbit Luck

Luck comes for Rabbits when they choose the right lover or partner. They can also find luck by buying or from selling art, antiques, exotic clothing, and décor to wealthy customers.

The Rabbit Elements

THE WOOD RABBIT (1975)

Wood Rabbits are conventional, intelligent, quiet, and modest, with compassionate natures, so they often help others who are less fortunate, and they sometimes do this in secret. They may find careers in sports and athletics, or as investigators or social workers.

THE FIRE RABBIT (1987)

These Rabbits are artistic and creative, but they are highly strung, emotional, unusual, and probably psychic. The medical professions appeal, as do alternative therapies. Fire Rabbits are cheerful, popular, and devoted to their partners and children.

THE EARTH RABBIT (1939, 1999)

These logical Rabbits want quiet lives, and they need to feel secure, so they are careful with money. They value education for themselves and their children, and they appreciate family life. Logical and sensible, they want ordinary jobs and uneventful lives.

THE METAL RABBIT (1951, 2011)

These unusual people might be into antiques or collectibles, but they may also surround themselves with junk. They need their own company at times and to be with friends at other times. They protect their friends and family and can be possessive.

THE WATER RABBIT (1963, 2023)

Water Rabbits are sensitive, romantic, caring, and easily upset. They live unconventional lives, maybe as creative people or as travelers who don't put down roots. They may never have wealth, preferring to experience life than to store anything up.

The Nature of the Dragon

Years: 1940, 1952, 1964, 1976, 1988, 2000, 2012, 2024

Polarity: Yang

Key attribute: Spiritual wisdom

Worst attribute: Tactlessness

The Dragon is the only mythological creature in Chinese astrology, and it is a symbol of China itself. It represents success and spirituality, and it is considered to be a lucky sign. This mythic creature represents transformation and spiritual knowledge and has unlimited potential. Dragons can take on major projects and carry others along with them, as others respect them for their ability. They are generous, conscientious, capable, good-natured, and wise. All the Dragon types seem to be excellent at home décor and do-it-yourself jobs, and they will take on quite complex building work, even though they don't actually choose careers in those fields. Dragons can be show-offs, and they are not above exaggerating their achievements. Still, their confidence evaporates when they meet someone more successful than they are—even if the success is in a completely different arena.

Dragons can be kindly folk who counsel those in trouble, and they have a spiritual nature that gives them an otherworldly glow. However, they also can be outspoken, arrogant, and just plain nasty on occasions. If someone stands in their way, they can turn into something that is the opposite of their everyday nature by lying, cheating, and being absolutely ruthless.

Under normal circumstances, Dragons have high standards for themselves and others, and they can be particular and demanding. Despite this, their charisma draws others to them, and they never disappear into the background. Dragons have an artistic streak, and they are particularly drawn to music. Dragons have a wonderful sense of humor, and they are great fun to be with; they are intuitive, and many are psychic. Dragons are excellent with children and young people, and they make great parents. While not all that reliable, they never turn away any of their offspring who come to them for help.

Dragon Love and Friendship

Dragons make amusing friends whose sense of humor will keep everyone laughing, but they don't like staying in the same place or among the same people for long, so their friendships come and go. They are flirtatious—in some cases exceptionally so—but while others fall in love with them, Dragons simply enjoy the flirtation for its own sake. They can be promiscuous, so they don't make great marriage partners, and they particularly dislike those who want more than they can offer. What they want above all things is to be admired. Having said that, Dragons retain the affections of their ex-lovers.

- Compatible for love with the Rat, the Horse, and the Monkey.
- Friendship or love with the Rooster, the Snake, and another Dragon.
- Incompatible with the Ox and the Rabbit.
- Signs that have no particular effect one way or another are the Tiger, the Goat, the Dog, and the Pig.

Dragon Careers

Dragons are risk-takers who have no patience with the cautious, slow, long-term approach to business, and they excel in fields where panache and flair are required. Dragons are ideal teachers and instructors, but they can also find careers in acting, crafts, arts, and music because they love an audience. They work hard and are reliable, turning up and doing the job even if they are sick or unhappy. Some Dragons may find work in the religious fields, and they can be as ambitious and successful as church ministers as in any other profession. Many find work in the psychic sciences.

Dragon Health

These active and energetic people don't suffer much from health problems, but their tendency to overdo everything means they may strain or even tear their muscles, tendons, and ligaments. Boredom is their enemy, so if they find themselves coping with too much routine, it will give them headaches and other stress-related problems. They need a change of scene from time to time.

Dragon Luck

The Chinese consider Dragons lucky, but they are also intuitive, so they can sense the right investments to take up and which to avoid.

The Dragon Elements

THE WOOD DRAGON (1964, 2024)

Wood Dragons are intelligent, inventive, and creative but often eccentric. They are lucky and will make a comfortable lifestyle and enjoy a long and happy life. They are not keen on married life, preferring friends, occasional lovers, and their own company.

THE FIRE DRAGON (1976)

These Dragons are clever and competitive; they have hot tempers and a determination to have their own way. They possess considerable charm, are never dull, and can be great fun to be with, but they are self-absorbed and prone to accidents.

THE EARTH DRAGON (1988)

These Dragons are talented and clever, but they know it and think they are right about everything. If they marry for love, their luck will grow, and they will become wealthy and successful, but if they marry for status and money, their lives will become a mess.

THE METAL DRAGON (1940, 2000)

These folks are keen on status, wealth, and the jet set, but if they don't make as much money as others, they may get eaten up by jealousy. They are blunt and opinionated, but their charm smooths this problem. Their worst fault is stinginess.

THE WATER DRAGON (1952, 2012)

Water Dragons are academic; they read a great deal and are often very knowledgeable, but being somewhat big-headed, they don't like advice from others. They make wonderful mediums, psychic counselors, or religious leaders. They need freedom.

The Nature of the Snake

Years: 1941, 1953, 1965, 1977, 1989, 2001, 2013, 2025

Polarity: Yin

Key attribute: Amiability

Worst attributes: Arrogance, easily irritated

Snakes are said to be the wisest sign of the Chinese zodiac, and they are usually intelligent, decisive, stylish, and eloquent. They love variety because they have a low boredom threshold. They don't even have much time for idle chatter, as they find it tiresome. They are excellent psychologists who can see what is going on inside the most complex person. Snakes are honorable, fun-loving, helpful, kind, and diplomatic until someone upsets them; then they can become surprisingly nasty. Snakes make good friends, but unforgiving enemies, and they never forget a hurt.

These folk look good and live in clean and tidy homes, they spend a lot on their homes, and they can be fussy about appearances. They are lucky where property is concerned, so they may live in one place and rent out another. They are good to their partners and they will bend over backward for their families and friends, but not so much for strangers, because they aren't especially idealistic or humanitarian. They may even be fonder of animals than they are of people, and I have noticed that cats, in particular, take a real liking to them.

Snakes are artistic and creative; thus, they may take up hobbies such as craftwork or sculpture. Most Snakes are good with young people, and some work as teachers, especially in some spare-time activity, such as music, singing, dancing, or art.

Snakes are relatively ambitious and fine while winning, but they become sore losers and can be unpleasant if someone overtakes them. They are snobbish and arrogant, but also pessimistic, and they can be worriers, which can affect their health, although this may not show on the surface.

Snake Love and Friendship

These independent people don't need the approval of others, and they regard it as beneath them to take other people's views into account. A Snake's greatest dread is becoming totally dependent on someone else, while appearing foolish or weak is almost shameful. Snakes are flirtatious, seductive, attractive, and sexy, and they can easily attract partners, but they choose those who are unusual or unconventional. They won't accept lies, and they are truthful themselves. They make good parents, but they won't stand for nonsense from their children. Some Snakes are ostentatious and competitive where status is concerned; they can irritate in-laws and other relatives in this way.

- Compatible for love with the Rooster and the Ox.
- Friendship works with the Rat, the Rabbit, the Dragon, the Goat, and the Dog.
- Incompatible with the Tiger and the Pig.
- Signs that have no particular effect one way or another are the Snake, the Horse, and the Monkey.

Snake Careers

The Snake can cope with administrative jobs, and they are diligent and well organized. They are practical and sensible but better with people than with technology, so teaching and training come easily to them, as do all forms of sales work. They are self-motivated, so they do well in self-employment. They love to travel and may own rental property in overseas countries, or they may travel for the sheer pleasure of it. Some work in the travel trade, especially for airlines. Snakes may work in politics, public relations, as businesspeople, psychologists, astrologers, and archeologists. In short, they prefer an interesting job to a mundane one.

Snake Health

Snakes run to extremes, so they have either excellent health or dreadful problems. They aren't interested in the opinions of others, and they aren't approval seekers, so their stress levels are pretty low. They can overwork and worry about money, so they need a routine job and a good income. Their lungs and hearts are not strong, so they should get out into the countryside or walk by the seaside as often as they can.

Snake Luck

Snakes find that unusual jobs or lifestyles bring them luck, and they can also be lucky by doing business in countries other than the one they usually inhabit. When jobs, companies, or partnerships go downhill, Snakes should jettison them immediately rather than keep trying to fix them because luck is not on their side in these situations.

The Snake Elements

THE WOOD SNAKE (1965, 2025)

Wood Snakes don't make changes without a good deal of consideration, because they are cautious and they worry about their financial security. They hate crowds and mess but are fascinated by intrigue and history. These Snakes are flirtatious, attractive, and sometimes fickle.

THE FIRE SNAKE (1977)

These Snakes are ambitious, dominant, self-possessed, arrogant, and opinionated. They love being around influential people, but they may make bad choices that they regret later. The Fire Snake is a little too self-centered for success in love relationships.

THE EARTH SNAKE (1989)

These Snakes are extremely determined and into long-term goals, so they work hard and do well in life, yet they need love and an understanding partner. They thrive with order and precision and can become wealthy, especially in property dealings.

THE METAL SNAKE (1941, 2001)

Metal Snakes are talented and gifted, but they can drift due to a lack of direction. They make enemies due to their pride and dishonesty. They never forgive enemies, but they can be loyal friends. Males like younger women and females like influential older men.

THE WATER SNAKE (1953, 2013)

These quiet Snakes are fastidious, astute, intelligent, and pragmatic with a dry sense of humor. They are ambitious, charming, and lucky, and they love to be near the source of power. They are intellectual and cool, and they like being with others of the same type.

The Nature of the Horse

Years: 1930, 1942, 1954, 1966, 1978, 1990, 2002, 2014, 2026

Polarity: Yang

Key attribute: Sociability

Worst attributes: Moodiness, abusiveness

Horses work hard and do whatever they can to make a good living, look after their families, and pay off their mortgages. They are really good with people, and for that reason, they often work in sales, in liaison jobs, or in medicine as doctors or specialist nurses. They are charming, cheerful, and fun to be with. People enjoy talking with Horses because they are intelligent, interested in everyone and everything, and non-judgmental—at least in public. What they say about others in private can be a different matter. These logical, honest people are sensible and capable, and if they are in the right mood, they can be helpful, kind, and loving. Horses make great hosts, and they love to be popular, so they join social clubs and raise money for charities. They are restless and love to be on the move, so they may travel for pleasure, business, or both, leading them to work in the travel trade.

If Horses don't receive the appreciation, respect, and admiration they desire, they can be sulky, hot-tempered, argumentative, or impatient and sarcastic, and some give others the silent treatment. A downside of this sign is that they are very talkative—they may pass on gossip and secrets. Another attribute is stubbornness, because they don't change their minds very easily and won't listen to reason. However, their most outstanding attribute is their reliability and ability to finish everything they start, so one can be sure they will complete any job once they have put their minds to it.

Horse Love and Friendship

Horse personalities enjoy being in love, but it takes a lot to sweep them off their feet. They love new relationships and thoroughly enjoy preparing for weddings and other romantic celebrations, sometimes forgetting that they actually have to live with the person once the celebration is over. They won't give up a demanding job or a way of life that they enjoy for the sake of their lover, and some can be miserly. Horses are quite sexy, needing to make love frequently. Their hot tempers can terrify their children. Many of them are better as friends than as life-partners. They are kind, helpful, and they make excellent counselors to those who need advice.

- Compatible for love with the Tiger and the Dog.
- Friendship with the Dragon, the Snake, the Monkey, the Rooster, and the Pig.
- Incompatible with the Rat, the Ox, and the Rabbit.
- Signs that have no particular effect one way or another are the Horse and the Goat.

Horse Careers

Horses work hard and look after their families, and they can work very long hours. They may become professional sportspeople or dancers, and they love to keep moving, so they may work with horses or in the racing business. They are good with their hands, so design, engineering, tailoring, and so forth are good occupations, but they might also work in construction, or as explorers, actors, artists, or in advertising. Their best jobs are definitely those involving inspiring people, liaising with them, or as salespeople. They are never lazy, and they don't leave jobs half-finished. They love to impress people with their ability and want their bosses to be pleased with them.

Horse Health

This is a strong sign that can throw off illness reasonably easily, but their tendency to ignore health problems and stay at work when ill can damage them. All the Horses I know have the kind of choleric hot tempers that eventually give them strokes and heart attacks, so they need to calm down. They don't do well with spicy or oily foods, which upset their digestion, especially their small intestines.

Horse Luck

Horses are luckier if they are born in the winter than in the summer, but they are hard workers, so they usually make their own good fortune anyway. Horses can be lucky by inheriting property, money, or goods.

The Horse Elements

THE WOOD HORSE (1954, 2014)

Wood Horses usually prefer country life to urban sprawl because they need space. They are sociable, friendly, and cooperative, bright and slightly unconventional. They are intelligent, freedom-loving, and very resilient, and able to recover from problems.

THE FIRE HORSE (1966, 2026)

Fire Horses can be too hot to handle. They are flamboyant, charismatic, and ingenious, but they are also rebellious and highly volatile. They love a fight, but they are also idealistic, loyal, and great employees.

THE EARTH HORSE (1978)

Even after thinking things through, these Horses are often confused and need guidance, which they hide under bossiness. They prefer the company of friends more than the company of relatives. Young Horses are wild, but they are fine when older.

THE METAL HORSE (1930, 1990)

These stubborn and self-centered Horses love variety, travel, and thrill-seeking, so they may not settle into stable relationships. They make or inherit money, so they can usually afford to live the good life. They love to argue, to show off, and to shock others.

THE WATER HORSE (1942, 2002)

After a difficult childhood, these Horses are vulnerable, and they dislike chaos or arguments. They love to travel; they may be sporty and they are competitive. They talk well and are good listeners, but they may not want secure and steady relationships.

The Nature of the Goat

Years: 1931, 1943, 1955, 1967, 1979, 1991, 2003, 2015, 2027

Polarity: Yin

Key attribute: Sensitivity

Worst attributes: Depression, pessimism

According to some, the Goat is said to be the worst sign to be born under, but this is an old superstition that isn't borne out by fact, because all the signs have advantages and disadvantages. These people are thoughtful, studious, reserved, or even shy, although they try to hide their timidity from others. Goats are kindhearted, good-natured, patient, and reliable, and they are known to be dutiful people who can take on an enormous workload. Some believe Goats can literally work themselves to death, but the truth is that they can only put up with a certain amount of pressure before they become sick with stress-related complaints. Goats are often found working in the arts, the media, as writers, or in professions involving healthcare.

Goats are the artists of the zodiac, and their artistic streak can make itself known in a variety of ways, such as dancing, writing, acting, and design. They are dreamy and deeply sensitive, but they disguise their sensitivity with humor, self-deprecation, or perhaps by putting on a display of indifference. Others turn to Goats when they need comfort and help, so the Goats can become the target of parasitic people who drain them of their reserves. In time, Goats learn to avoid these people and to protect themselves. Goats can't cope with bullies, confrontation, or vulgarity.

As children, Goats don't need strict discipline, because they want to please their parents and teachers, and above all, they want to be loved. This was a sign of righteousness and duty to the family in ancient China, and Goats put up with their fates without complaint. The vices of this sign are pessimism, insecurity, depression, a troubled love life, and self-pity. Some may drink or harm themselves when downhearted.

Goat Love and Friendship

Goats are very attractive, both in their looks and due to their kindly natures, but they don't believe they are nice looking or particularly interesting to others. They are stylish, graceful, and often lovely, but also unassuming. Their values are based on a spiritual rather than a material plane, and they are totally lacking in envy or malice. With these characteristics, it is easy to see why Goats are likely to be in demand and considered a worthy mate by so many people. They are drawn to those of a similar creative or original nature.

- Compatible for love with the Horse, the Rabbit, and the Pig.
- Friendship with the Dragon, the Snake, the Monkey, and the Rooster.
- Incompatible with the Rat, the Ox, the Tiger, and the Horse.
- A sign that has no particular effect one way or another is the Dog.

Goat Careers

Despite their gentle natures and inability to stand up to bullies, Goats can be amazingly successful, and they can make others green with envy. They are excellent communicators who are also artistic, which may show up in the form of singing, playing musical instruments, dancing, acting, or writing. Goats spot gaps in the market and exploit them, which can lead to success, and they do all this without much ambition, other than wanting to be happy in their work.

Goats have a deft touch with accountancy and the complexities of tax and bureaucracy. They can also do well as civil servants, as the backroom boys and girls in the world of politics, or they may choose to help others by going into alternative therapies, astrology, or work as travel agents, salespeople, or social workers.

Goat Health

These gentle people attract what one might call "motherly" partners who like to look after them, which is a good thing because they are prone to diabetes, which leads to a host of problems if not kept under control. The eyes are weak spots because their vision can become cloudy due to glucose collecting in the lenses, and they can suffer from cataracts and macular degeneration. Other affected areas are the heart and the liver. They need to keep their weight down and to eat carefully.

Goat Luck

Goats are said to be the unluckiest sign of all, as they follow rather than lead. However, Goats can achieve considerable success either by using their artistic and accountancy talents or by seeing gaps in the market. When they become successful, they take people by surprise, often attracting envy from those who had previously written them off.

The Goat Elements

THE WOOD GOAT (1955, 2015)

Deeply thoughtful people who tend to be nostalgic, sentimental, good-humored, and compassionate, these Goats can also be too trusting and, therefore, can be taken advantage of by less scrupulous people. These Goats mother everyone whom they love.

THE FIRE GOAT (1967, 2027)

These Goats are more like Rams as they are courageous, ready to take the initiative and defend their territory. They may be dramatic and fond of causing scenes, but they aren't clever with money, so they can lose their wealth. They are thinkers and dreamers.

THE EARTH GOAT (1979)

These creative and hard-working Goats may be defensive at times, but they are also honest, trustworthy, and stable, so they gain prosperity through their own efforts. They hate deceit, so they may be too honest for comfort within a relationship.

THE METAL GOAT (1931, 1991)

Metal Goats have more confidence than others and are refined and honorable, but they can still be easily hurt. These Goats can be moody, jealous, and possessive, while also being clannish, very family-oriented, and not fond of social situations that put them among strangers.

THE WATER GOAT (1943, 2003)

Water Goats need love and approval and will do anything to get it! They hate to upset anyone and are content to follow the flock. Despite their unassuming nature, they are excellent communicators, and they achieve great success in their chosen field.

The Nature of the Monkey

Years: 1932, 1944, 1956, 1968, 1980, 1992, 2004, 2016, 2028

Polarity: Yang

Key attribute: Ambition

Worst attributes: Arrogance, know-it-all nature

These people think and act quickly, are intelligent and sometimes exciting, but they are easily bored and need variety. They love to have a nice home and will work hard to have the best house in the best neighborhood, but they also enjoy going out and about, either by working long hours, belonging to clubs, enjoying busy social lives, or traveling a great deal. They love to meet new people and impress others, so they become popular wherever they are, and they are often the center of attention. They loathe boring people or being bored themselves. They need the latest gadgets, a good car (or two, if possible), and a partner who looks good and who won't let them down in public. Monkeys need exercise, in the form of either sports or walking their dogs, but they also need time to read because that is how they relax.

Monkeys are quick to catch on to the latest new idea, and they are remarkably intuitive, so their inner minds can operate simultaneously with their conscious brain. They read a lot, watch educational programs on television, and know a great deal about everything, and their excellent memories mean they retain much of what they take in. They can be amusing and even funny when they want to be, but they can also be very nasty, sarcastic, and amazingly uncaring to those who know them or love them when they are in a bad mood. Some are jealous, spiteful, restless, and even dishonest, but most are fine, if somewhat exhausting, to be around.

There are many legends about Monkeys in China and throughout the East, and this isn't surprising as these animals are so like us. Tradition sees the mischievous, resourceful, and intelligent Monkey as the likable trickster.

Monkey Love and Friendship

Monkeys like the idea of being in an exciting relationship, and they will likely have several partners during their lifetime. They prefer an inspiring or even unconventional partner, and they have no time for whiners or fusspots. Those who get involved with Monkeys must expect them to be busy with other things for much of the time and even to disappear from time to time, so tolerance is required. Monkeys can move on relatively quickly, and they prefer to remain friends with their previous lovers if possible. They make terrific, if demanding, parents, and their worst fault is to push education, sports, outside interests, and anything else they can think of onto their overloaded children.

- Compatible in love with the Rat, the Horse, and the Dragon.
- Friendship or love with the Dog, the Goat, and the Rabbit.
- Incompatible with the Snake, the Pig, and the Tiger.
- Signs that have no particular effect one way or another are the Ox, the Monkey, and the Rooster.

Monkey Careers

This ambitious sign does well in business, and they don't fear taking risks or doing things on a super-huge scale so that they can become international success stories. They love to be in charge and don't have enough patience to flatter their superiors or even treat them with much respect. This makes them ideal for self-employment and running their own show. They can be innovative and ahead of the crowd, so anything to do with the online world or new ideas suits them well.

Monkeys are restless, so they can become bus, cab, or delivery drivers or traveling salespeople. These hardworking folk can work in the media, the travel trade, as theatrical agents, or even as manual workers, but they will make a success of all they do.

Monkey Health

Monkeys can overdo their work and worry, and they can spend too much time driving or sitting at a computer. They need exercise, rest, and time alone to recharge their mental and emotional batteries. All the Monkeys I know have problems with their bowels, such as polyps, colonic inflammation, or even cancer. Their lungs may be weak, so they shouldn't smoke.

Monkey Luck

Monkeys don't do well at school and can be written off as failures by their families, but they soon find an avenue that suits them, and they land on their feet whatever they do. They may then become ruthless, often succeeding because they don't worry about anybody else's opinion.

The Monkey Elements

THE WOOD MONKEY (1944, 2004)
After a restless youth, Monkeys become shrewd workers who don't mind taking risks. Where love is concerned, they make mistakes at the start, possibly by jumping into relationships without enough thought, but they find happiness later.

THE FIRE MONKEY (1956, 2016)
Imaginative and clever, these bold and energetic Monkeys can be great leaders, although bossy ones. They can be hot-tempered, stubborn, and fond of their own opinions, competitive, and suspicious, but they do well in creative lines of work.

THE EARTH MONKEY (1968, 2028)
These Monkeys are generous and protective to those they love but totally unfeeling to outsiders. They are bright and knowledgeable, and they like others to appreciate that fact. When they apply themselves to work, they can become hugely successful.

THE METAL MONKEY (1980)
These Monkeys seem cool, independent, and sophisticated, but inwardly they are ambitious, hardworking, and creative. They are hard to influence and must do their own thing. They are deep thinkers who need a sound belief system.

THE WATER MONKEY (1932, 1992)
The soft and diplomatic nature of these Monkeys makes them successful agents or representatives. They are slightly idealistic and will help others. They have friends everywhere and marry partners who won't embarrass them or behave foolishly.

The Nature of the Rooster

Years: 1933, 1945, 1957, 1969, 1981, 1993, 2005, 2017, 2029

Polarity: Yin

Key attribute: Entertaining

Worst attributes: Vanity, critical

Roosters were thought to be military types, probably because they liked impressive uniforms, medals, and banners. These days they find their way into the media to show off and get paid for it! Even if a Rooster is not in the public eye, he or she likes to be in the spotlight, and always dresses well and looks good. Underneath the entertaining outer manner, there is shyness and a lack of self-confidence. Some are exhibitionists, and others are actors who take on roles that allow them to be someone else. Something may have gone wrong in their childhood, making them insecure and apt to overthink things and worry too much. They are hard workers, and they believe in their own judgment and opinions, which often prove to be correct.

These people don't have great childhoods, and they may not succeed at school, so people don't realize how intelligent and well-read they are. They know a great deal about their favorite subjects and such things as art or music. They may be intellectuals, but they don't flaunt this, so others may not realize just how brainy they are.

In ancient Chinese writing, the Rooster is described as having five "virtues": an intelligent mind, a martial spirit, courage, benevolence, and reliability. They are said to be honest and truthful, and the Rooster symbol can supposedly ward off evil.

Rooster Love and Friendship

Roosters are attractive and very flirtatious, and they are unlikely to settle down into domesticity early in life owing to their independent natures along with their hatred of routine and boredom. Male Roosters have many girlfriends with whom they stay on good terms, while females are far more sensible and happy to be in a relationship. Both sexes love a good time and a good laugh on nights out with friends. Roosters are cheerful, charming companions who can be reliable and responsible with the right partner, but they have a hidden jealous streak, which means that while they allow themselves plenty of leeway, they don't like it if their partner starts looking around.

They make the best of friends, are supportive and caring toward others, and are always there when someone needs a shoulder to cry on or even a bed for the night.

- Compatible for love with the Snake, the Ox, and the Dragon.
- Friendship with the Tiger, the Horse, the Goat, and the Monkey.
- Incompatible with the Rabbit, the Dog, and the Rat.
- A sign that has no particular effect one way or another is the Pig.

Rooster Careers

Roosters are highly intelligent and extremely capable, but they need to do things at their own pace and don't like making instant decisions. They have a dramatic streak that may lead them to work in the entertainment industry or as lawyers. Still, they are also happy to work in the hospitality industry, where their charming manner and ability to chat with anybody comes in handy. Their personal standards are very high, and while they can make money, they love to spend it, so they may not become rich. Frankly, they prefer to enjoy life, vacations, and having a good time rather than pile up money in the bank. Roosters are particularly suited to the media, public relations, the law, arbitration, commercial sales, and politics, while some become beauticians or clothing designers. They are also thought to be suited for careers in the military.

Rooster Health

Roosters need exercise and rest as well as companionship and an excellent social life. Their stomachs and intestines are sensitive, so they need a varied diet without too much spice or junk food. They may also suffer from hemorrhoids. Many seem to have bad feet, possibly suffering from heel spurs, ingrown toenails, tight ligaments, trapped nerves, bunions, and so on. Their lungs aren't strong, so they shouldn't smoke.

Rooster Luck

Roosters are considered so lucky that the Rooster symbol is used as a charm to ward off evil. They are talented but not demanding or pushy, so they need a lucky break from time to time if they are to get anywhere in life; however, their friendliness and popularity mean that friends often jump in to lend them a hand when needed.

The Rooster Elements

THE WOOD ROOSTER (1945, 2005)

These Roosters are great communicators, to the point that they can talk their way into or out of anything. They are optimistic, decent, and honest, and while they can be demanding, they are never unfair.

THE FIRE ROOSTER (1957, 2017)

These Roosters succeed in everything they do because they want to be seen as remarkable and to stand out from the crowd. They are charming leaders who have plenty of followers and friends. Their finances improve as they get older.

THE EARTH ROOSTER (1969, 2029)

These Roosters have more sense than other types; they are intelligent and sensible with money, but they can be moody and opinionated, so they may find it challenging to retain love relationships, despite their need for emotional security.

THE METAL ROOSTER (1981)

These Roosters make great lawyers because they are great at arguing a case, along with being determined and hardworking. However, they are abrasive, moody, and complicated, so personal relationships may never be as successful as their careers.

THE WATER ROOSTER (1933, 1993)

Communication is the name of the game here, and these Roosters can be found in the world of computing, the media, and as salespeople. They can be indiscreet, though, so telling them too much isn't a good idea. They are at home in the worlds of art and music.

The Nature of the Dog

Years: 1934, 1946, 1958, 1970, 1982, 1994,
2006, 2018, 2030
Polarity: Yang
Key attribute: Loyalty
Worst attribute: Critical worriers

Dogs are loyal, honest, and courageous, and their sense of right and wrong makes them champions for those who are badly treated. They can always fight for causes. However, they are most likely to fight on behalf of their relatives and friends. They are good to older relatives and even get on well with their in-laws, and they rarely break a promise or act in a disloyal way. Their high standards mean they can be critical of both their own behavior and that of others, so they don't hesitate to point out other people's failings, which doesn't exactly endear them to fellow workers. These people are generally wise and sensible, and they make great listeners and counselors. They can be worriers who think the glass is half-empty.

When Dogs come across people who are in difficult situations, they do all they can to help. As adults, they need peace and quiet in their homes and, if possible, also at work. They relieve their sensitive nerves by enjoying hobbies such as art, music, gardening, and cooking, but they can be too fond of eating, especially sweet foods, and drinking too much wine. They may have weight problems later in life.

Dog Love and Friendship

Apart from Water Dogs, this sign is not likely to play the field because they are happiest in settled relationships with supportive partners who can boost their occasionally flagging confidence level. These people love nothing better than a happy family, a nice home, and peaceful relationships with their relatives and children. They are patient with children and will happily play with them or make things for them, and they can teach them a great deal about scientific subjects.

Dogs are loyal, supportive, and good listeners, but they only open their hearts to others once trust has been established. They need calm and capable partners, and they need to curb their oversensitivity and tendency to see attacks and offense where none exist. Above all, they need to be loved.

- Compatible for love with the Tiger, the Horse, and the Rabbit.
- Friendship with the Rat, the Snake, the Monkey, and the Pig.
- Incompatible with the Ox, the Goat, the Rooster, and the Dragon.
- A sign that has no particular effect one way or another is the Dog.

Dog Careers

In some cases, dogs can be leaders and even executives, but they are best in ordinary jobs where they do their work, go home at the end of the day, and put the jobs out of their minds. They are good with their hands, and they are often very skilled, so they make excellent builders, farmers, electricians, carpenters, and manufacturers. They have a knack for mathematics and science, so they can be found in engineering and laboratories. Their artistic and musical gifts mean they might work as picture restorers or even makers of musical instruments. They are happiest when they know what to do from one day to the next. They put their minds to their jobs and can be relied on to do things properly and finish what they start. Dogs can work in teaching, the law, social work, as doctors, nurses, counselors, campaigners, gardeners, or clergy.

Dog Health

Dogs can overeat, and they love such foods as cake and ice cream, so they are in danger of gaining weight. They may have problems with their circulation, urinary systems, prostate glands, and kidneys, so they should limit alcohol. Dogs suffer from arthritis in later life, so they need to keep moving as much as possible and keep their weight down to avoid too much pressure on their knees and hips. Dogs get headaches when stressed out.

Dog Luck

Dogs are associated with protection and loyalty, so doggy statues are often set outside the doors of houses to keep bad luck out.

The Dog Elements

THE WOOD DOG (1934, 1994)

It is advised for these Dogs to beware of strangers and to take precautions against theft. They love working on their homes and gardens, and they tend to be honest and decent, family-minded and cooperative.

THE FIRE DOG (1946, 2006)

These Dogs are likely to make a success of themselves and to be noticed. They love their homes and families, but they also love changes of scene, travel, and fun. They are independent spirits who can be difficult at times.

THE EARTH DOG (1958, 2018)

Well organized and systematic, these Dogs can run successful enterprises, sometimes working so hard that they wear themselves out. They are great advisors and very good with their families, but they can overspend and sometimes get into financial difficulties.

THE METAL DOG (1970, 2030)

These Dogs are so idealistic that they can take up causes. They are also good family members, although they can be overbearing and quick to take offense over nothing. They need to be in charge because they don't like taking orders from others.

THE WATER DOG (1982)

Restless and amusing, these dogs are entertaining, good company, and quick to empathize with others. Their charm makes them attractive, and they easily make friends. They settle down late in life and become good family members.

The Nature of the Pig

Years: 1935, 1947, 1959, 1971, 1983, 1995, 2007, 2019

Polarity: Yin

Key attribute: Kindness

Worst attribute: Gullible

Pigs are known for their honesty and kindness, and they will give help and support to anyone who needs it, so this, along with their non-judgmental attitude, makes them popular with others. Pigs can be insecure and short of self-confidence, but they get over this in time. They are hard workers who are also quick-minded and intelligent, and they make a success of themselves later in life. Pigs are good with young people, so they are good parents and outstanding teachers, who can work with young people in such areas as the Scouts. Once they overcome their shyness, they can talk about many subjects that interest them. They have few friends but many acquaintances who appreciate their cheerful good natures. Hardworking Pigs are calm, reliable, straightforward, and gallant.

Pigs are not attuned to business, and their trusting nature makes them likely to be swindled, used, and deceived. Yet, despite this, Pigs represent wealth, family fortune, and abundant possessions, so they are considered a good omen in China. The Pig's eagerness to be a friend and to help others makes them sometimes overstep the mark or appear silly. Their worst fault is that they can be lustful in a sexual situation. Male Pigs can take their desire to experiment a bit too far and become perverted or even depraved.

Pig Love and Friendship

Pigs want to love and be loved, and they can fall hard, which makes them vulnerable to those who wish to use them or take advantage of their good nature. They need to be sure that when they find someone, it is the right person for them. Fortunately, they are intelligent, and they don't make the same mistake twice. Pigs are quite intuitive, and they can see what others are up to, so they soon pick up on infidelity or other problems. A practical but fairly subtle partner will appreciate their sensitivity and academic minds, and with the right person, Pigs are happy, helpful, kind, and loving—and very sexy.

- Compatible for love with the Rabbit and the Goat.
- Friendship with the Rat, the Ox, the Tiger, the Dragon, and the Horse.
- Incompatible with other Pigs, the Snake, and the Monkey.
- Signs that have no particular effect one way or another are the Rooster and the Dog.

Pig Careers

Pigs are good teachers, but they can also find work in hospitals and the caring professions. Some work in the worlds of antiques, music, or even the law, but others are good with computers or working as librarians, researchers, or gardeners. They can work in printing or publishing as they have an artistic eye. These people are not ambitious, preferring to have a job and a good balance between their work and home lives. They like a comfort zone and being part of a team to the greasy pole of ambition and success. The Pig's natural caution and lack of business instinct keep him or her away from risky projects, sales work, or anything to do with money. Some may be professional athletes, particularly as members of teams, and some are drawn to careers in the military. They can also be people who work in practical jobs, such as carpentry or engineering.

Pig Health

Pigs can be put upon by others, which leads to resentment and occasional explosions of fury. They need to be less accommodating and avoid bullies, or they will build up too much cholesterol, which leads to heart trouble. They can also have problems with the bowels and bladder. However, for the most part, they are a healthy bunch, just needing rest and some "me time" when they can dance, play sports, listen to music, paint, read, and relax.

The Pig Elements

THE WOOD PIG (1935, 1995)

These Pigs are helpful and kind, and they may become social workers or health aides. They are not usually fortunate in any form of business, but they can excel in athletics or something creative, such as design or printing.

THE FIRE PIG (1947, 2007)

These highly-strung personalities are artistic, unusual in many ways, and possibly overly emotional. They find work in the caring professions or as complementary therapists of some kind. They are good family members, but they can bully others on occasion.

THE EARTH PIG (1959, 2019)

These Pigs are sensible and capable but not ambitious, although they are happy to support an ambitious partner. They are family-oriented people who want ordinary lives. They aren't clever with money. They can overdo eating and drinking at times.

THE METAL PIG (1971)

Pigs are not usually ambitious, but these are. They can be domineering, crafty, and unpleasant in their desire to have things their own way. They are outgoing and sociable, but they need time alone. They love and protect their family and friends.

THE WATER PIG (1983)

These Pigs love to travel, to see new places and meet new people. They are sensual and sexy, and they may overdo this or perhaps eat or drink too much. They are very creative and artistic, and they prefer to work in an artistic field rather than to make money.

✳ ✳ ✳

(4)

ANNUAL
FORTUNES

Every year is linked to one of the twelve animal year signs, and this has consequences for all of us, making some years lucky and others difficult, depending upon the sign involved.

One quick way of assessing your own fortunes is to check the polarity of your sign, because a year that shares your polarity is easier to cope with than one that does not. For instance, if you were born during a yang year, you will love the speed of events and changeable nature of the yang years, while you will consider yin years slow and boring. If you were born during a yin year, you will appreciate the slower pace and relative peace of yin years, finding yourself disconcerted and ill at ease during the hectic and volatile yang years.

Here is a reminder of the list of polarities:

The Polarities

Rat: Yang	Ox: Yin	Tiger: Yang	Rabbit: Yin
Dragon: Yang	Snake: Yin	Horse: Yang	Goat: Yin
Monkey: Yang	Rooster: Yin	Dog: Yang	Pig: Yin

Some Chinese people consider the return of your own animal sign to herald an unlucky year, but others believe that since the energies inherent in the year match your own energies, it is easier for you to cope with whatever comes your way.

In addition to the effects each sign has on individuals, each animal also has its own nature and energy that can affect events around the world. I have briefly listed these at the start of each animal sign section in this chapter.

The Year of the Rat in General

Years: 1936, 1948, 1960, 1972, 1984, 1996, 2008, 2020

A good year for new projects, enterprise, and opportunity, but those in positions of authority will have problems. Arts and creativity will succeed. This year suits those who work hard or who are trying to survive in difficult situations.

The Rat in the Rat Year

According to some, your own year is not a good one, but Rats usually achieve success and happiness, along with love and passion, in their own year. They just need to be sure they don't push their luck or upset others, as that will result in a few harsh lessons.

The Ox in the Rat Year

Oxen will work hard this year, but they will see good results from their efforts. It is a good year for friendship and intellectual connections, while Oxen will enjoy stretching their minds. New romance is unlikely, while current relationships will just carry on as usual.

The Tiger in the Rat Year

This is a good year for networking and for making new friends, but it isn't a great time to get involved in risky ventures. Tigers who have put something aside for rainy days will likely need it this year.

The Rabbit in the Rat Year

Although Rabbits will have more opportunities to express themselves and be more adventurous than usual, there will also be pitfalls for Rabbits who don't watch their backs. Friends could let them down, and con artists will abound.

The Dragon in the Rat Year

The way forward for Dragons is to use their brains rather than pushing others around, but they can expect to be happy this year. Others will appreciate them, and they can expect joy and happiness in family life, with lots of people in and out of their homes.

The Snake in the Rat Year

This is a challenging year for Snakes, with potential for health problems, difficulties at work, and even having to give up on a job and be out of work for a while. Relationships are all right, but finances are not, and worries abound.

The Horse in the Rat Year

Horses would do better to work on their own self-development than to get involved in the schemes of others, as that may lead to insecurity and worry. Horses should put their own plans on hold, or they'll end up fighting battles on all fronts!

The Goat in the Rat Year

Goats will be more energetic and much more successful during the Rat year as they make significant progress in their professional lives. However, finances might be under strain now, so it isn't the time to take risks or buy anything that isn't necessary.

The Monkey in the Rat Year

If Monkeys have felt that they were missing out on big breaks in previous years, this year's news will be very welcome and provide opportunities. Finances will improve, and anything to do with children will be positive and well-favored.

The Rooster in the Rat Year

This will be a challenging year for Roosters, with finances being strained. Even if Roosters make a profit, it will soon drain away again. Relationships may be difficult, and work will be tough. The best thing is to take care and avoid risky ventures.

The Dog in the Rat Year

Dogs should focus on the home and family this year and avoid getting involved in business schemes. Others may boast about their money and possessions, which will irritate Dogs, but they should just get on with their own lives and tune out the noise.

The Pig in the Rat Year

Pigs should work out what they want to achieve this year and then go all out to get it. It is not a time for sitting around but for getting on with things, albeit slowly and sensibly. It is a year of optimism and happiness for the most part.

The Year of the Ox in General

Years: 1937, 1949, 1961, 1973, 1985, 1997, 2009, 2021

This is not a great year for speculation or risky ventures, but one to stay with traditional ways, with safe investments and keeping one's nose to the grindstone. Things may go slowly during much of the year, then speed up right at the end of it.

The Ox in the Ox Year

Some say that one's own year is an unlucky and unhappy one, but this isn't necessarily so because in this case, there will be several new opportunities that Oxen might wish to consider. These will affect both the near and the distant future.

The Tiger in the Ox Year

This is a frustrating year for Tigers, as things will move too slowly for their taste, and they will also have to watch their words, because conflicts and arguments are likely to arise. Tigers must not get into unnecessary contests with others as they will lose.

The Rabbit in the Ox Year

Relationship matters will go well, and there may be new babies coming into the family circle, but there will be many problems as far as work is concerned. It would be best to pay attention to mundane chores and to learn from experience.

The Dragon in the Ox Year

Dragons might find this year slow and somewhat boring, but it is an excellent time to work their way through long-term projects and finish what they start. They should hold back, though, because bold and chancy moves won't succeed.

The Snake in the Ox Year

Snakes can follow their instincts and take advantage of the opportunities that come their way. The slow pace of events will suit them, and they can make steady progress. It is just a matter of keeping a cool head and putting one foot in front of the other. Finances will slowly improve.

The Horse in the Ox Year

Love and romance will be turbulent and unpredictable, but Horses will find their working life all right if they just keep going with their usual routine. There will be a lot of hard work, but Horses will feel as if they are getting somewhere.

The Goat in the Ox Year

Goats will learn valuable lessons this year by living through exceptionally difficult times. Family life may be trying, and Goats may have more work than they can cope with; however, it will be all right if they keep going and don't make major changes.

The Monkey in the Ox Year

Monkeys are capable of sustained effort, but they aren't enthusiastic about it, so they may become bored and fed up with their workload. However, they will have the opportunity to learn new skills this year, which will stand them in good stead.

The Rooster in the Ox Year

Roosters need to seize every chance that comes their way this year, as it will be a time of success and achievement. There will be a need to exercise common sense, though, and if something doesn't look right, it probably won't be. Otherwise, things are all right.

The Dog in the Ox Year

The best thing for Dogs to do is to focus on practicalities this year and leave idealism and even charity for another time. Dogs need to toe the line and fit in with others as much as possible and just do their work without expecting too much fun.

The Pig in the Ox Year

This is a year for quiet, confident progress, as the hard work that Pigs put in will eventually be well rewarded. The downside is that Pigs will need to avoid overindulgence, keep an eye on their waistlines, and avoid bad habits.

The Rat in the Ox Year

Rats will work hard this year, but they don't mind this, especially as the outcome of all their efforts will be successful. It might be a challenging year for lonely people, although friendships will be more successful than a search for love.

The Year of the Tiger

Years: 1938, 1950, 1962, 1974, 1986, 1998, 2010, 2022

There is nothing peaceful about this animal, so everybody can expect a roller-coaster year in which anything could happen. Some will find this year too turbulent for their peace of mind, but those who like excitement and change will be happy.

The Tiger in the Tiger Year

According to some, your own year is likely to be bad, but that isn't necessarily so. It is a time to throw caution to the winds and take a chance on business and life. Romance and love relationships of all kinds will bring happiness this year.

The Rabbit in the Tiger Year

Despite the turbulence of this year, Rabbits will prosper. They may find mentors or helpers who help them adapt to new circumstances, and Rabbits will end the year in a much more fortunate situation than initially.

The Dragon in the Tiger Year

Work and business will forge ahead quickly, and finances will pick up, but there is a chance that Dragons will become self-important, which won't earn them respect. Love and relationships will be pleasant, and there might be some exciting vacations.

The Snake in the Tiger Year

This is going to be a busy year, and Snakes will have a lot on their plates. Snakes must take care during the first few months, as they could have accidents that leave them struggling. The best thing is to take things one day at a time.

The Horse in the Tiger Year

There will be a lot of fun for Horses this year, with holidays, partying, and major celebrations, but this will empty their bank accounts and leave them short if they are not careful. They must avoid overconfidence or leaping without looking.

The Goat in the Tiger Year

This will be a challenging year that could give Goats a great deal of anxiety.

Goats need to keep their wits about them. However, allies could offer help, and more experienced and courageous Goats will make headway and do so quickly.

The Monkey in the Tiger Year

Monkeys will use their intelligence to act as negotiators or advisors this year, and while it may be a challenging year in many ways, it will provide some unexpected strokes of luck. Monkeys must avoid becoming lazy or taking things for granted this year.

The Rooster in the Tiger Year

Things will move very quickly this year, and even though Roosters like to be busy, it might be hard to manage their lives. There will be changes at work and in the family, and everything will be up in the air for a while. Roosters should try to relax when possible.

The Dog in the Tiger Year

Luck is on the side of the Dogs this year, whether in finance or an opportunity for adventure. Those who like to stir up revolution or get involved in sports or charitable fundraising will have a lot of fun. However, Dogs will be more gullible than usual.

The Pig in the Tiger Year

Turmoil and excitement don't suit Pigs, resulting in unsettled times, but their laid-back nature means they will ignore a lot of the surrounding chaos. Pigs need to keep their ambitions under control and their plans under their hats this year.

The Rat in the Tiger Year

Rats will need to cope this year with difficult situations that are likely to arise, and circumstances that suddenly become unstable and insecure. However, Rats are natural survivors, so they will use their brains and talents to find the best way out of danger.

The Ox in the Tiger Year

This is not the best year for Oxen, and major changes should be left for another year if that is possible. All Oxen can do is work hard at the important things, be pleasant enough, and not try to make new friends at work or elsewhere.

The Year of the Rabbit

Years: 1939, 1951, 1963, 1975, 1987, 1999, 2011, 2023

This is a peaceful year with an emphasis on art, design, and music, so it is a time to enjoy these things. Charities will do well because those who have plenty will want to help those who do not, and the world's finances will also pick up.

The Rabbit in the Rabbit Year

Some say that one's own year is never a good one, but this will not be the case for the Rabbit this year, as even risky ventures will pay off. There won't be much money around, though, so Rabbits will need to count the pennies and watch for those who might take advantage of them.

The Dragon in the Rabbit Year

This year, dragons should take things slowly and not expect much to happen, because it will be a quiet year. Others won't appreciate Dragons who become over-enthusiastic, and they may try to put them in their place. It's best to enjoy a quiet year.

The Snake in the Rabbit Year

At last, Snakes will feel more confident and find both the time and the money to enjoy life's pleasures. It's a great time to get out more, to see a little more of the world and to do it in style. Snakes must avoid deviousness and be straight with everyone.

The Horse in the Rabbit Year

Horses might find themselves in front of audiences, giving presentations or in some other way in the public eye this year. Some colleagues might react by becoming envious, but this shouldn't hold the Horses back from making their mark.

The Goat in the Rabbit Year

Goats are creative, and this is a year in which their artistry and creativity will be greatly appreciated. Goats will make new friends, enjoy a better social life, and have some much-needed fun. Family life will be pleasant, and children will bring much joy.

The Monkey in the Rabbit Year

Monkeys in business will do well this year, but there will be opportunities to relax and allow tensions to wash away in between. Monkeys will find their reputation on the rise and their influence growing, and they can expect help from others.

The Rooster in the Rabbit Year

This is likely to be an irritating year, and Roosters would do well to maintain a low profile and not show off their achievements or the things they own. Practical matters will go well enough, but life won't be particularly exciting.

The Dog in the Rabbit Year

This is a good time for Dogs to start new ventures or try their hands at new hobbies. New love may also be in the air for some. However, Dogs should avoid too much chasing around and pursuing something impossible to catch.

The Pig in the Rabbit Year

There will be excellent opportunities for growth at work and an improvement in personal life and family life this year. Indeed, there may be new additions to the family soon. Pigs must avoid being too generous, though, or they will become short of money.

The Rat in the Rabbit Year

Rats will have to watch their backs this year, as enemies might emerge and take it upon themselves to attack the Rats. These little rodents will fight hard and probably win in the end, although it will be a stressful and challenging learning curve.

The Ox in the Rabbit Year

This is a time to maintain the status quo and not rush into anything. It should be a good year for relationships, although a change of attitude might be advantageous. Holidays and indulgences are possible, provided these are not too extravagant.

The Tiger in the Rabbit Year

If Tigers avoid showing off and keep to the straight and narrow, this will be a year of success. Tigers will progress well at work, their finances will pick up, and they will find themselves leaving others behind. Love relationships will be all right too.

The Year of the Dragon

Years: 1940, 1952, 1964, 1976, 1988, 2000, 2012, 2024

This is a year of extremes and unexpected events for everybody. Those who are entrepreneurial and think big will prosper this year, and everybody should find life exciting, although it might be a bit too exciting in some cases.

The Dragon in the Dragon Year

Some believe that one's own year is never a good one, but this isn't the case here, although this will be a roller-coaster year with a few ups and downs. Dragons will look impressive, and they should be able to earn more money this year.

The Snake in the Dragon Year

Snakes can cope with the unpredictability of the Dragon year, although they must consider their own needs first and foremost and not get too involved in the problems of others. Snakes can't take on too much, and they must keep their priorities straight.

The Horse in the Dragon Year

This should be a good year for career matters and a busy social life, and there will be a heightened sense of excitement. The only problem is that Horses might be tactless or apt to talk too much and speak out of turn.

The Goat in the Dragon Year

Goats need to save money for emergencies toward the end of this year, but as long as they are sensible, they will be all right. Other aspects of their lives will be fine, and they will feel less burdened by problems than they have for some time.

The Monkey in the Dragon Year

Travel is advised this year, and Monkeys will do well at work; they could become more successful than usual. It will be a costly year, but Monkeys are high earners, so they can afford the extra expenses this year will bring.

The Rooster in the Dragon Year

This is a good year for Roosters, when they can make an impression and receive approval. They should abandon caution and go for whatever they want, whether in love, business, or sports, as anything competitive or new will be fine.

The Dog in the Dragon Year

About the best thing one can say is that times of trouble can be character building, as life is likely to be stressful at times this year. Dogs will have to learn something new this year or find out how to cope with new things that are particularly difficult.

The Pig in the Dragon Year

Pigs need to be more outgoing and not keep their talents hidden. Many Pigs have a sneaking suspicion that something underhanded is going on, and they may become caught up in misunderstandings, so they must take care.

The Rat in the Dragon Year

It may take a while, but Rats will find their feet this year and begin to relax as the surrounding atmosphere improves. It will be easy for Rats to find love, exciting new relationships, and lasting friendships as the year progresses.

The Ox in the Dragon Year

Oxen will need to keep a cool head this year, as Dragon years are notably volatile. Tension and stress will take their toll, and the Oxen who get into fights will lose their battles. It's best for Oxen to keep their heads down and to use their common sense.

The Tiger in the Dragon Year

These two animals have much in common, and neither of them likes to waste time, so Tigers can expect to move speedily ahead, both at work and in their personal life. They may have to play second fiddle to others, though they must maintain a professional attitude.

The Rabbit in the Dragon Year

This is not the best of years for Rabbits, and they must avoid taking unnecessary risks or getting involved in chancy ventures. Rabbits should get on with their work and keep away from the turmoil created by others. Relationships range from peaceful to nonexistent.

The Year of the Snake

Years: 1941, 1953, 1965, 1977, 1989, 2001, 2013, 2025

Snakes hide up trees, in swamps, or in the undergrowth, so this year will bring revelations on both a large and a small scale. Politicians and national governments will feel the full glare of publicity, and scandals will come to light.

The Snake in the Snake Year

Despite the view that we have bad luck in our own animal year, that will not happen to Snake people this year. They will have luck where relationships are concerned, their children will do well, and they can get ahead in their profession if they put in the work.

The Horse in the Snake Year

It may not be easy for Horses to resist temptation this year, so whether it is food, alcohol, or sex that causes problems, it will be hard to avoid them. Horses are usually sensible, but their common sense seems to desert them this year.

The Goat in the Snake Year

Goats should express their creativity to the full this year, and their talents and hard work will be appreciated, so they will feel less nervous and insecure than they usually do. Their love lives will be more exciting and passionate this year as well.

The Monkey in the Snake Year

This is a year of mysteries, muddles, and secrets for Monkeys that could make jobs, relationships, or life extremely hard to manage. Something that is going on behind their back will emerge and create a significant change in their point of view.

The Rooster in the Snake Year

Creative matters will go well this year, and there will be success at work as well. Best of all, this is an excellent year for love, when problems are ironed out and happiness is all around. Others will envy Roosters this year, but Roosters won't care.

The Dog in the Snake Year

Dogs should avoid intrigue this year, as this will only make them anxious. They should consolidate what they have achieved and avoid going too far out on a new limb, and they must be absolutely honest and avoid illegal dealings.

The Pig in the Snake Year

There is an air of disharmony around, giving Pigs cause to worry and be anxious. Caution needs to be the watchword this year as business deals will not be above board and romance might also be fraught with difficulties.

The Rat in the Snake Year

Rats must keep their eyes open and their wits about them, because they may find themselves among people who don't have their best interests at heart. Rats must always be honest and truthful, even if other people are not.

The Ox in the Snake Year

Oxen will now be able to reap the rewards from work they have done in the past in this easy and comfortable year. Finances will improve, and savings will begin to increase, while those in business will find themselves making a nice profit.

The Tiger in the Snake Year

This will be a slow year for Tigers, so they will have to be patient and just go with the flow. Relationship matters will be stuck in the mud, and work will be okay but not exciting. Tigers must learn to relax and let things happen at their own pace.

The Rabbit in the Snake Year

While Rabbits may struggle with their love life this year, work will go reasonably well. It is a good idea to take a training course or get involved in education now, but even this might lead to Rabbits being on the receiving end of jealousy.

The Dragon in the Snake Year

Dragons may have a feeling of being in the right place at the right time, which relates to work issues and love and relationships. Nevertheless, it would be good for Dragons to keep a low profile and keep their opinions to themselves.

The Year of the Horse

Years: 1930, 1942, 1954, 1966, 1978, 1990, 2002, 2014, 2026

The Horse year favors those who are honest. Integrity will be essential at this time, because secrets will emerge, and scandalous celebrities and dubious politicians had better beware. Plans will come to fruition if they are well thought out.

The Horse in the Horse Year

Some believe that we don't have a good year when it is our own animal year, and that seems to hold true this year, because Horses might find life hard going at times. Life will be tricky, and lessons will be learned, but troubles don't last forever.

The Goat in the Horse Year

This is an up-and-down year, with financial improvements and an easier life, but there will be dramas and upsets in the family circle and possibly at work as well. Goats will have to keep as calm as possible under the circumstances. Travel is advised, though.

The Monkey in the Horse Year

Things will happen very quickly this year, but it would be best for Monkeys to keep quiet and follow the rules. They should not try to stand out or impress others; instead, they should just do their jobs, run their families, and avoid spending money unnecessarily or running up debts.

The Rooster in the Horse Year

Roosters need to take care of their health this year, eat sensibly, do some exercise, and dump bad habits. It isn't a bad year, but things may go so quickly that they leave Roosters running to catch up. There will be a need for hard work at times.

The Dog in the Horse Year

This should be a good year for exploring and traveling, as new horizons will open up now. Although there will be worries at times, Dogs should be able to earn or make more money, bringing some relief. Meditation or long walks will calm their nerves.

The Pig in the Horse Year

Pigs will have to work hard this year, but they will be rewarded for their efforts. Despite a spell of analysis and self-doubt, Pigs will find their fortunes improving as the year goes by. Those who have been let down in love will find new partners this year.

The Rat in the Horse Year

This will be an expensive year that gets worse if Rats have overspent during previous years and gone into debt. Rats who have been careful will cope, but there won't be much left over, as chances for gain vanish and problems arise.

The Ox in the Horse Year

Oxen need to maintain a steady path through the turbulence of the Horse year, but hard work and persistence will pay off, and past efforts will be rewarded. It is advisable to push ahead, though, and not to sit back and become complacent.

The Tiger in the Horse Year

The Horse year is ideal for adventurous Tigers, as everything will go their way, whether financially, in business, or in their love life. The only setback is that Tigers can become big-headed, which will annoy others.

The Rabbit in the Horse Year

This is a good year for romance and friendship, but Rabbits must avoid getting too involved in the problems of others or taking on lame ducks. If Rabbits focus on their own world, they will cope well with the increasing speed of events.

The Dragon in the Horse Year

Passion takes over this year, but let's hope it doesn't develop into an obsession. There will be plenty of good luck around, and life will be exciting and changeable. This is a great year for sports, travel, and adventure if Dragons keep a sense of balance.

The Snake in the Horse Year

It's important that Snakes have good people around them, because work and business are likely to be trying this year, and very little will go according to plan. Snakes must be honest in their dealings because others are only too happy to misrepresent them.

The Year of the Goat

Years: 1931, 1943, 1955, 1967, 1979, 1991, 2003, 2015, 2027

Traditionally, the Year of the Goat favors anything that will benefit humanity, so social and medical advances are likely. The artistic side of the Goat will probably find expression in radical new fashion trends and mass movements, especially those that promote peace.

The Goat in the Goat Year

According to some, our own year is never a good one, but this should be a good year for love relationships and for passionate ones. Goats can be themselves, free from the complaints, demands, and criticisms of others. Some will make major decisions.

The Monkey in the Goat Year

This will be a much better year and a time when Monkeys can put the unpleasantness of the past two years behind them. Prosperity and success are on the way, and problems will be easy to sort out. Monkeys will feel happier and more settled this year.

The Rooster in the Goat Year

Roosters need to take time for family and friends this year, as they may need their help or just want to enjoy their company. Minor problems may grow into big ones, so anything that looks like potential trouble requires immediate attention.

The Dog in the Goat Year

Love, relationships, and family life will be pleasant and happy this year. Creative or artistic work or hobbies will be very successful now. There may be a few money worries, but they shouldn't be too serious, and Dogs tend to worry anyway.

The Pig in the Goat Year

This might be a quiet year, but at least it is a happy one, especially for romance and partnerships. Pigs will be contented and relaxed, and they can expect a few family celebrations and other events that will be enjoyable and memorable.

The Rat in the Goat Year

A good year for Rats, as they will be able to forge ahead with confidence. Creative work will go well, and Rats may enjoy the artistry of others by going to shows, art galleries, and so on. This is a time for love and friendship.

The Ox in the Goat Year

Life will be a bit weird at times, and some things will be hard to understand. Love and romance will be rather good this year and lovemaking will be particularly good, but it won't be a great year for business or finances.

The Tiger in the Goat Year

Even Tigers sometimes need a quiet year to go on an inward journey, notice the things going on around them, and be patient. It is no good trying to stand out from the crowd now, or Tigers may find themselves out of favor.

The Rabbit in the Goat Year

Rabbits can expect a blessedly peaceful year now, with lots of giggles with friends and social events of all kinds. Finances could be better, but Rabbits will be happy to do simple things with like-minded friends that don't involve a great deal of expense.

The Dragon in the Goat Year

Dragons who work in the media, theatre, or the arts will do very well, but even those with more conventional careers will find new talents. Life will pick up, and there will be new friends who appreciate the talented Dragons.

The Snake in the Goat Year

This is not a great year for risk-taking, and Snakes must be careful about whom they trust. If new lovers ask for loans, it would be best for Snakes to give them a bit of money and tell the lover to keep it rather than lend a considerable sum, which will not be returned.

The Horse in the Goat Year

Horses who have been unsettled for some time will find it easy to settle down this year, which might mean finding a good home or a better job. Some may decide to become parents this year, partly due to being in a happy and comfortable relationship.

The Year of the Monkey

Years: 1932, 1944, 1956, 1968, 1980, 1992, 2004, 2016, 2028

The best-laid plans will go awry—often before they've even started. Adaptability is the key to success this year, because the wheel of fortune is spinning wildly. Quick profits can be made but also lost, so nervous types should keep calm and avoid change.

The Monkey in the Monkey Year

Some say that your own year is not good, but this year should be all right. Monkeys can expect to join new groups and clubs, take up new sports and interests, and make new relationships, while business will also be very successful.

The Rooster in the Monkey Year

Complications will arise in relationships, and there will be misunderstandings all around. Plans will go out the window, so Roosters are probably best off just going with the flow and not trying to make changes or make much sense of anything.

The Dog in the Monkey Year

This will be a lucky year for Dogs with windfalls coming their way and opportunities to try new activities or for adventure. Even a small wager would be successful. If that is not enough, love and romance are likely to be enjoyable and exciting now.

The Pig in the Monkey Year

It is good that Pigs are intelligent, because they will need to keep on top of things this year. There are too many intrigues going on, and Pigs will struggle with some of them. Pigs should stick to their own path and avoid risks.

The Rat in the Monkey Year

This will be a happy and stress-free year, when Rats can expect to have fun and to enjoy a measure of success. Opportunities will open up, and Rats will find themselves in demand during this exciting year. Rats should travel and make new friends this year.

The Ox in the Monkey Year
The best aspect of this year is the likelihood of a new love affair. The situation at work or in business will be turbulent and unpredictable, and it will be hard for Oxen to adapt swiftly to the changes that are going on around them.

The Tiger in the Monkey Year
Although this is a better year for Tigers, it is also tricky, as they could find themselves among untrustworthy people who let them down. However, if Tigers use their creativity, this should lead to success at work and in home improvements.

The Rabbit in the Monkey Year
The Monkey year is a tricky one, and it isn't likely to be great for Rabbits. The best they can do is to get on with their lives, work quietly, and keep away from troublemakers. It might be best for Rabbits to enjoy painting, singing, and similar hobbies.

The Dragon in the Monkey Year
Things will happen at great speed this year, and there could be a lot to do. While this is exciting, it is also unnerving, because this will be a year of unpredictable events. Dragons should maintain a steady course and not try too many new things.

The Snake in the Monkey Year
Snakes must be cautious this year and not take anything or anyone at face value, because they will spend a great deal of time struggling to work out what's really going on. Snakes mustn't get involved in anything that isn't absolutely straightforward.

The Horse in the Monkey Year
This is a year of fun and doing many things for the first time, and Horses might even consider a wager or invest in some new venture. It is a reasonably lucky year, so all these things should work out well. There will be entertainment and friendships galore.

The Goat in the Monkey Year
A common curse goes, "May you live in interesting times," and these times will be too interesting for comfort. Goats should take up meditation, walks in the country, yoga, gardening, or any relaxing hobbies. They should make time to rest more.

The Year of the Rooster

Years: 1933, 1945, 1957, 1969, 1981, 1993, 2005, 2017, 2029

This year will be great for those who want to advance at work, achieve a higher status in society, and improve their reputation in any creative field. The Rooster brings a sense of order and organization, so a new era will be established where there was chaos.

The Rooster in the Rooster Year

Although some believe your own year might not be a good one, this will be just fine, as Roosters will be able to enjoy themselves this year. Fortunately, Roosters can earn money, because they may spend a bit too much this year.

The Dog in the Rooster Year

There may be too much going on this year, and Dogs could feel tired at times. Dogs are idealistic, but some of their ideas are too impractical, and this year, it is common sense that will be needed. Dogs need to stay positive and make the best of things.

The Pig in the Rooster Year

Developing knowledge and skills is the best way forward for Pigs this year, and some of this might be in an artistic or creative field. Pigs will need to budget carefully and avoid overspending on luxuries if they want to stay on the straight-and-narrow.

The Rat in the Rooster Year

Work may be a pain this year, but Rats will find their love life compensating for this by being exciting and enjoyable. Rats may have to give up on a particular job or project and look around for something more useful and productive to do.

The Ox in the Rooster Year

After a few difficult years, Oxen can now look forward to a new adventure of some kind. Oxen need to brush up their image, spend some money on their home and appearance, and enjoy life, although love matters may not be so successful.

The Tiger in the Rooster Year

Tigers are good at promotion and public relations, which is just as well because this is a good year for it, and problems will turn out to be minor ones. Tigers will find their love lives picking up, with many opportunities for dating and long-term love.

The Rabbit in the Rooster Year

This year, the best thing to do is keep a steady course and not get involved in anything risky or costly. It isn't a good year for money, and this will worry Rabbits. They should enjoy watching or playing sports or getting into artistic or creative hobbies.

The Dragon in the Rooster Year

Dragons will be able to seize opportunities, and their finances will prosper, but their private lives may take a real nosedive. It is not a year to make promises, and it may even be a time to question current commitments or bring something to a close.

The Snake in the Rooster Year

Snakes looking for a lovely home or improving the one they are in will be able to do so because this will be a much better year for these folk. Plans will move closer to reality, and new friends will offer sound advice and practical help.

The Horse in the Rooster Year

This year, settling down is the name of the game, as Horses may find themselves in steady relationships and good jobs now. They may take out mortgages or start businesses this year, and it should all work out well if they are sensible.

The Goat in the Rooster Year

There may be a new start for Goats, and romance will go well, but Goats will find themselves on the receiving end of unpleasantness from others which will get them down. Goats will need time alone for their sensitive nerves to settle down.

The Monkey in the Rooster Year

The family will be important for Monkeys this year, and there could even be an addition to the family group soon. Monkeys should take what others tell them with a pinch of salt and ignore boastful people, and they should offload difficult people now.

The Year of the Dog

Years: 1934, 1946, 1958, 1970, 1982, 1994, 2006, 2018, 2030

This is a good year for relationships and working partnerships, but there is a hint of danger this year, as everyone will need to insure their homes and possessions and make sure they are secure. It is not a great idea to take anything on trust this year.

The Dog in the Dog Year

Some believe that one's own year is never good, but this year should be fine for Dogs, as their ideas will work out well and others will be impressed. Everyone will want to hear what Dogs have to say, and they will have reason to feel proud of themselves.

The Pig in the Dog Year

On one hand, Pigs might want to join others in a fundraising or charitable venture, but on the other hand, they shouldn't overload themselves with responsibilities that don't have much to do with them. They need time alone in the countryside and peace.

The Rat in the Dog Year

This should be a successful year for Rats who will either be promoted or find new jobs that are better than their old ones, and their income will improve too. Sadly, there may be problems in relationships, and they may have to work hard to keep love alive.

The Ox in the Dog Year

It is not a good idea for Oxen to dig their heels in and refuse to accept new circumstances, as a more flexible attitude will be the best way forward. Oxen will want to travel to new places and have new experiences, which will be good for them.

The Tiger in the Dog Year

The revolutionary zeal of these animals will bring luck to Tigers, and their ideas will be in fashion. They will come up with clever ideas and inventive schemes. Work will be extremely productive, and friendships and love will be pleasurable and fun.

The Rabbit in the Dog Year

Lonely Rabbits should focus on dating this year, because there is a good chance they'll find someone to love. Business ventures will be worrying, and Rabbits might even start to believe that others are out to stab them in the back. They must relax more.

The Dragon in the Dog Year

Dragons with happy partnerships and a great home life will be all right this year, but they must be absolutely faithful to their lovers. Selfishness won't work, so Dragons will have to learn to put others first and benefit from this.

The Snake in the Dog Year

This should be a good year with improvements in finances and practicalities, so some will open a new business or improve an existing one. However, despite all the hard work, Snakes should take some time out to have fun and relax.

The Horse in the Dog Year

Love, romance, and committed relationships should work well for Horses this year. Everything else will be all right as well, if not exactly thrilling or exciting. It would be best to plod on in the same way as usual and to put the needs of others first.

The Goat in the Dog Year

Goats must avoid getting involved in other people's messes or conspiracies. They may have to do without luxuries now, but Goats can cope with this, although they won't enjoy it much. They need to look after their own interests and not help others too much.

The Monkey in the Dog Year

The message here is to keep going because tenacity will pay off. This could be a trying year, but persistence and hard work will pay off. Relationships could be strained, and everyone around could be overworked, harassed, worried, or irritable.

The Rooster in the Dog Year

Roosters need to keep the lines of communication open this year, as they will be in demand by everyone, sometimes for weird reasons and usually at the least convenient time. There will be conflicting requirements and a considerable expenditure of energy.

The Year of the Pig

Years: 1935, 1947, 1959, 1971, 1983, 1995, 2007, 2019

This year brings a feeling of celebration and pleasure, so there will be pleasant vacations, great outings, and a chance to buy nice clothes and look good in them. Romance, love, and family life will all go well, and Pigs will be cheerful and happy this year.

The Pig in the Pig Year

Although some say one's own year is never a good one, this year will come as a relief to Pigs. Some will move to a better area or start a new family, while others will enjoy career opportunities, but some will find themselves embroiled in a secret affair!

The Rat in the Pig Year

This should be a lovely year, with an enjoyable social life and a lot of fun. Finances will improve, and this will be the start of a more successful phase, and even investments will work out well. Sports and other leisure activities will be successful and enjoyable.

The Ox in the Pig Year

Oxen will want to improve their homes and private lives this year, and they will have the opportunity to do so. Professional and personal life will improve, and Oxen will be happy if they do their own thing without worrying about what others want of them.

The Tiger in the Pig Year

Although there will be some opportunities for success, this is the time to enjoy a busy and active social life. Tigers may spend more money than usual, and they should relax when they see others doing better than themselves as they will soon catch up.

The Rabbit in the Pig Year

There should be celebrations and happy family events this year, and romance will also go well. Finances will improve, and there may even be a small windfall that Rabbits should spend on clothes, accessories, their hair, and their appearance in general.

The Dragon in the Pig Year

Nothing much will change this year, so if Dragons are happy, they will continue to prosper, but those who long for change will have to wait a bit longer. Dragons will have to avoid arrogance in order not to upset important people or their bosses.

The Snake in the Pig Year

There will be obstacles placed in the way of Snakes this year, so they must watch out for them. There will be fun, but Snakes should try to avoid over-indulging in food or alcohol or giving in to other temptations, or there will be a price to pay later.

The Horse in the Pig Year

It isn't a good year for jumping into anything without much research and planning, as complications will arise even in good situations. Horses should exercise caution this year and not allow their naturally impulsive natures to take over.

The Goat in the Pig Year

This will be a year of success and happiness for Goats, and a chance for their creativity to shine, because others will appreciate their talent and imagination. If Goats keep their wants and needs within limits, they will be happy and relaxed this year.

The Monkey in the Pig Year

Monkeys need to avoid practical jokes, trickery, and mockery this year, and behave well and keep out of trouble. Other people will do well now, making Monkeys envious and angry at times. It's best to get on with things and wait for a better year to come.

The Rooster in the Pig Year

Roosters may find things coming a bit too easily today, which will make them wonder if everything is what it seems to be. Roosters know that nothing comes without trying, so this will make them feel suspicious and more cautious than they usually are.

The Dog in the Pig Year

This is a calm and relaxed year, when love relationships go well, and Dogs can expect to have some fun. There will be an emphasis on culture, so Dogs may enjoy music, art, literature, or being among intellectuals who spark their interest.

✴ ✴ ✴

PART II

THE POLARITIES, MONTH SIGNS, AND FOUR PILLARS OF DESTINY

5

THE LUNAR AND SOLAR NEW YEAR AND THE POLARITIES

Lunar and Solar Dates

Now that we're getting further into this subject, there is a serious complication that we just can't ignore, which is the situation surrounding the lunar and solar new year dates.

In chapter one of this book, I have given you the dates for each lunar new year, and almost everyone can use those dates to find their year sign. However, these dates move around from one year to the next, which makes life difficult for professional Chinese astrologers and Feng Shui practitioners. Therefore, Chinese astrologers use a solar new year date of February 4 for everybody.

I mention this because nearly all online software uses the lunar dates, which is what I expected to find when I checked this out, but I have now discovered that professional quality software uses solar dates.

This situation is only really a problem for "cuspy" people who were born around the end of January and the beginning of February, as they may find their year sign is one thing by the lunar system and something else by the solar system, and they will have an outer nature that is a mixture of both year signs.

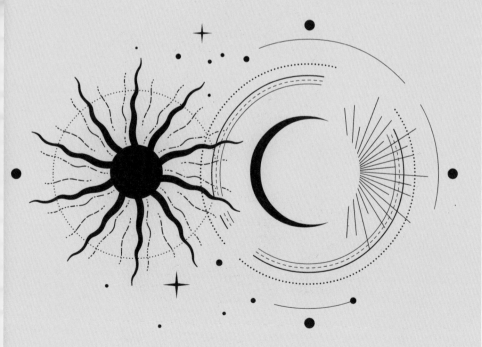

The Polarities

When yin and yang were worked out some 2,000 years ago, the northern half of China was said to be yin and the southern half was considered yang.

Yin became attached to the ideas of a northern climate of long winters, snow, and long nights. However, it also ruled sitting at home in front of a fire and eating soup, resting, and mending implements needed for farming and fishing once spring came around. Yin ruled mending, food preserving, and caring for children and small animals. On a larger scale, yin also ruled such things as working in banking and dealing with taxation and budgeting for local or national government. Yin rules trade, the movement of goods, salesmanship, and construction, along with arbitration, negotiating, and persuading.

Yang is associated with the hot southern areas of China, and hence with summer. Yang was associated with planting, animal husbandry, fishing, hunting, fighting off enemies, harvesting, and working hard, inventing things,

and making things happen. Also considered yang were warriors, explorers, pioneers, authority figures, leaders, and those who worked with big projects, such as engineers, designers, leaders, and activists—in short, spheres of life that were considered masculine and that required an impulsive and dynamic nature. Yang also meant enjoying long spells of hot weather—too hot at times—and lots of daylight even in the winter.

Yang	Yin
Male	Female
Sun	Moon
Light	Dark
Day	Night
Active	Passive
Hot	Cold
Summer	Winter

Yang People—Including Type A Personalities

Type A personalities are not common, but we tend to know them when we come across them. For instance, if we work for a large organization, it is likely that there will be one at its head. These people come from all kinds of backgrounds, but whatever start they had in life, they make a huge success of themselves. They often have a great deal of charm, but they are also ambitious, driven, capable, intelligent, ruthless, and lucky. We all know who they are because they are politicians, airline owners, tycoons, police chiefs, and even major criminals. They are in the news every day, and we love or hate them. Yang people are generally courageous and possibly foolhardy; they have chutzpah and are willing to take chances.

Rat: Yang

Ox: Yin

Tiger: Yang

Rabbit: Yin

Dragon: Yang

Snake: Yin

Horse: Yang

Goat: Yin

Monkey: Yang

Rooster: Yin

Dog: Yang

Pig: Yin

Yin People—Including Type B Personalities

Most people are Type B personalities who prefer to live ordinary lives and to avoid risky ventures, which suggests that most people have a fair amount of yin in their personalities.

A Bit of Both

However, each side of the famous symbol contains a dot within each side that represents a bit of the other polarity, so even yang people have a bit of yin in them and vice versa. Add to this the fact that nobody's personality is ruled by their year sign alone, because we all also have a month sign, a day sign, and an hour sign, so most of us are a mixture of yin and yang.

Alternate Years

Where the animal signs are concerned, the polarities rule alternate years, as per the chart on the previous page. Generally speaking, those born in a yang year will make more headway in yang years, while those born in a yin year will be less harassed and more relaxed during yin years.

6

MORE ABOUT THE ELEMENTS

The elements are an essential aspect of Chinese astrology that some consider more important than the animal signs. In ancient times, the Chinese believed that the elements were linked to ten gods, and they were the paths that allowed mortals to contact those gods and petition for their help when needed. Each element was linked to two of the ten gods.

The elements are often referred to as the heavenly stems, which makes sense when one considers their link to the heavens, while the animal signs are often referred to as the earthly branches, which link them to worldly concerns.

There are five elements, each of which rules two years, which is why you will often see the elements referred to as biennials. The first year of each element is always yang and the second is always yin. These ten items rule ten

years, but there are twelve animal signs, so it takes a total of sixty years for the whole system to rotate, by which time every animal sign will have been linked to every element. The technical name for this system is the *sexagenary* cycle.

SEXAGENARY CYCLE

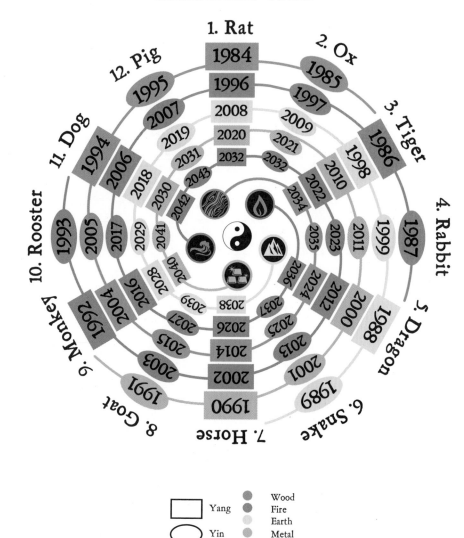

▢	Yang	● Wood
◯	Yin	● Fire
		● Earth
		● Metal
		● Water

Here are the elements and associated polarities with the Chinese names added.

Element	Polarity	Chinese Name
Wood	Yang	Jia
Wood	Yin	Yi
Fire	Yang	Bing
Fire	Yin	Ding
Earth	Yang	Wu
Earth	Yin	Ji
Metal	Yang	Geng
Metal	Yin	Xin
Water	Yang	Ren
Water	Yin	Gui

Here is a quick way of working out which element and polarity will operate during any year.
- If the year ends in 0 it will be yang Metal.
- If the year ends in 1 it will be yin Metal.
- If the year ends in 2 it will be yang Water.
- If the year ends in 3 it will be yin Water.
- If the year ends in 4 it will be yang Wood.
- If the year ends in 5 it will be yin Wood.
- If the year ends in 6 it will be yang Fire.
- If the year ends in 7 it will be yin Fire.
- If the year ends in 8 it will be yang Earth.
- If the year ends in 9 it will be yin Earth.

The elements have many correspondences, and the table below shows a few common ones.

	Wood	Fire	Earth	Metal	Water
Direction	East	South	Center	West	North
Season	Spring	Summer	Change of Season	Autumn	Winter
Shape	Rectangle	Triangle	Square	Oval	Wavy
Features	Eyes	Taste	Mouth	Nose	Ears
Taste	Sour	Bitter	Sweet	Pungent	Salty
Weather	Wind	Heat	Damp	Dry	Cold
Color	Green	Red	Yellow	White	Black or Blue
Planet	Jupiter	Mars	Saturn	Venus	Mercury
Feng Shui Animal Link	Azure Dragon	Red Bird or Phoenix	Yellow Dragon	White Tiger	Black Tortoise

The Element Cycles

I've chosen three well-known element cycles that I feel will be most useful for readers of this book. The idea is that you move from one element to the next, or in some cases, jump forward by two elements at a time, for the best outcome. A diagram is given for each cycle to show how this works.

The Creative Cycle

The image below shows the creative cycle, including a legend that relates to the system.

THE LEGEND

• Wood burns to create Fire.
• Fire turns to ash and nurtures the Earth.
• Earth contains ore that creates Metal.
• Metal allows Water to flow across it.
• Water nurtures trees to create Wood.

For instance, if you were born during a Wood year, you can expect success during two Fire years, because they immediately follow the Wood years, or if you were born in a Fire year, you could expect success during the two Earth years, because they follow the two Fire years, and so on.

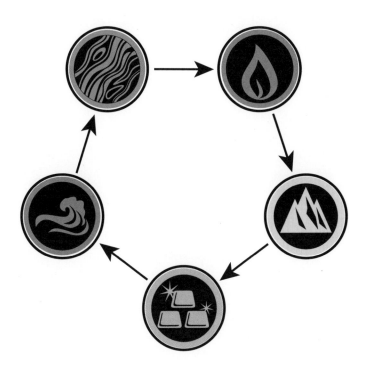

The Destructive Cycle

According to the system, when the element preceding the one that rules your year sign is in charge, you can expect to have a difficult time at work or in the home or both.

THE LEGEND

- Wood pollutes Water.
- Water rusts Metal.
- Metal pollutes Earth.
- Earth douses Fire.
- Fire burns Wood.

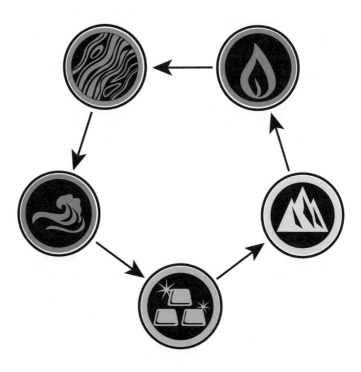

The Compatible Cycle

You can also expect to enjoy good years when the elements two signs ahead from your own are ruling.

Also, romance is likely to flourish with someone of your own element or someone born two elements ahead from yours. For instance, someone born in a Metal year should find it easy to get on with those born in Wood years.

THE LEGEND

• Wood gets on with Earth and Metal.
• Fire gets on with Metal and Water.
• Earth gets on with Water and Wood.
• Metal gets on with Wood and Fire.
• Water gets on with Fire and Earth.

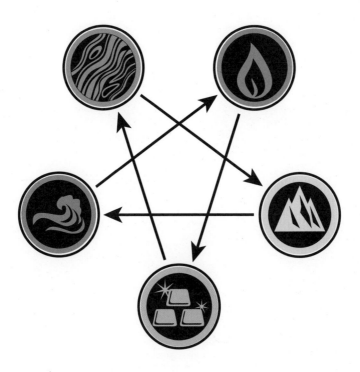

7

MORE ABOUT THE COMPATIBILITY OF YEAR SIGNS

Something that is worth bearing in mind is that the year sign is supposed to represent our *outer* personality. For more information about the year signs, let's start with a quick glimpse into each sign's characteristics, both positive and possible negative aspects.

Sign	Nature
Rat	Charming, clever, quick-witted, and appealing. Can overspend, hoard, or be wasteful.
Ox	Dependable, dexterous, thorough, sociable. Can be hot-tempered, fears competition.
Tiger	Rash, competitive, proud, fascinating, courageous. Unstoppable, fierce.
Rabbit	Friendly, gossipy, artistic, dislikes confrontation. Aloof, snobbish, fussy.
Dragon	Confident, lively, elegant, decisive, dramatic. Muddled, moves away quickly when bored.
Snake	Careful, possessive, family minded, needs a nice home. Seems clever but is actually naïve.
Horse	Sociable, sporty, active, loves travel, great salesperson. Intolerant, prejudiced.
Goat	Methodical, fastidious, clever, dislikes mess, artistic. Too soft and can't always cope.
Monkey	Inventive, risk-taker, agile, well-read, clever. Manic then depressed, needs admiration.
Rooster	Shrewd, clever, alert, punctual, showy, dramatic. Abrasive, competitive, extravagant.
Dog	Sociable, reliable, good to family, honest, loyal. Fussy, insecure, overthinks.
Pig	Hardworking, home-loving, practical, likes nice possessions.

Compatible Signs

There are four sets of animals, four signs apart from each other, that fall into compatible groups. People in each group have a similar nature, so they understand one another and get on well with one another.

- **Group One:** Rat, Dragon, and Monkey
- **Group Two:** Ox, Snake, and Rooster
- **Group Three:** Tiger, Horse, and Dog
- **Group Four:** Rabbit, Goat, and Pig

Compatible Signs

Opposites often attract. So when looking for love, we might find people of another group more interesting than those in our own.

The image below will give you an idea of how the system works.

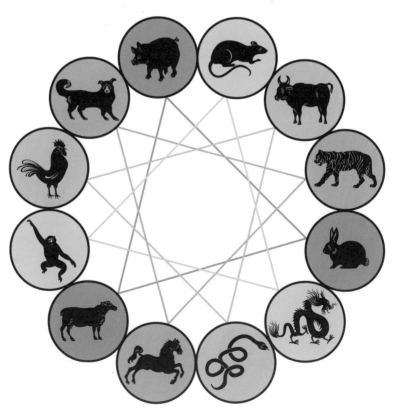

Group One—Rat, Dragon, and Monkey

The Active Group: People of these three signs are intense and powerful individuals who are capable of great good or great evil. They make terrific leaders, but each has a different approach. These signs are so capable that they are destined for success in whatever sphere of life they choose. They climb whatever ladder is available to them, whether it is the usual one of work and money or some kind of religious or social organization. They are ruled by a high, potent energy, and they can be unpredictable.

Group Two—Ox, Snake, and Rooster

The Thorough Group: These souls conquer the world through endurance, application, and slow accumulation of energy. Each sign is fixed and rigid in its opinions and views, but they are geniuses in the art of meticulous planning. They are hardworking, discreet, modest, industrious, loyal, punctual, philosophical, patient, and good-natured individuals who have high moral standards. At worst, they can also be narrow-minded and petty.

Group Three—Tiger, Horse, and Dog

The Hasty Group: These signs seek true love and are like-minded in their pursuit of humanitarian causes. Idealistic and impulsive, these signs follow their own drumbeat. Defiant against injustice, these signs also need large amounts of physical affection, and they also need loyal support for whatever interests them. They are productive, enthusiastic, independent, engaging, dynamic, and honorable. These three signs don't enjoy being dictated or lied to, but they will listen to someone they love or trust. They can be rash and stubborn.

Group Four—Rabbit, Goat, and Pig

The Gentle Group: The quest for these three signs is to be creative and classy. Their relatively calm natures give them great leadership abilities. They are artistic, creative, refined, intuitive, and well-mannered, and they are said to be the best lovers of the zodiac! They may not be wealthy or even particularly happy much of the time, but they are often resigned to their condition in life, and they can be strangely detached from all the chaos that goes on in the world. They are compassionate, caring, unique, gentle, self-sacrificing, obliging, sensible, empathetic, tactful, creative, and prudent. They can also be naïve, prone to worry, and pessimistic.

8

THE MONTH
SIGNS

The month sign is taken from the date of birth. The starting date for each month must have meant something to early Chinese astrologers, but the original logic has become lost over time. These dates are now commonly accepted for the start of each astrological month, so they are what we still use.

Dates for the Month Signs

Dates	Month Animal
December 7	Rat
January 6	Ox
February 4	Tiger
March 6	Rabbit
April 5	Dragon
May 6	Snake
June 6	Horse
July 8	Goat
August 8	Monkey
September 8	Rooster
October 9	Dog
November 8	Pig

You can discover how the month sign modifies your personality by going back to chapter three and reading the animal year sign but this time applying the information to your month sign. For instance, if your month sign is the Horse, read the Year of the Horse section.

✳ ✳ ✳

How Does the Month Sign Modify Your Personality?

If you were born during the year of the friendly, quiet, gentle, helpful Pig, this year sign would represent your outer personality, or how you appear to others. Being such a gentle soul, you could easily become the victim of those who love to push others around. However, if your month sign is the Tiger, Dragon, or Monkey, which represent your inner personality, your abusers would be in for a big surprise at how you react to that abuse. The month sign is as strong as the year sign, but it is not quite as obvious to others.

Monthly Forecasting

You can forecast what might happen to you during a particular month using the monthly signs as well. Say you want to see what February will hold for you in any year. Check out the list on page 117 and you will see that February is the month of the Tiger, so look in chapter four for the fortunes for your sign during the year of the Tiger and apply it to the month.

THE SNAKE IN THE RABBIT YEAR

Here is an example:

Jenny was born under the year of the Snake, but she wants to see how life will be for her during March, which will be the month of the Rabbit. She turns back to chapter four and checks out the fortunes for the Snake, and when she reaches the reading for the year of the Rabbit, this is what she will find:

At last, Snakes will feel more confident and will find both the time and the money to enjoy life's pleasures. It's a great time to get out more, to see a little more of the world, and to do it in style. Snakes must avoid deviousness and be straight with everyone.

An Ancient Luck Guide

This ancient guide works for everybody, not just people of any particular sign. It shows which month is traditionally lucky for a specific kind of activity. In the past, the month signs started at the winter solstice, which is around the 21st of December. But over time, calendar changes have pushed this date back to December 7, and it is now the traditional start to the month signs.

Month 1	
Month of the Rat	This is a favorable month for new projects, so try to generate new business and pay bills and barter for what you want to buy. Local travel will be all right, but long-distance travel is not advised, especially travel by boat. Avoid building, gardening, and work with heavy machinery. Don't touch your savings or stored food.
December 7 to January 5	
Jian—Establish	

Month 2

Month of the Ox	This is not a good month for accomplishing anything important. However, it is a brilliant time to clear away clutter and do some cleaning, wash your car, take your clothes to the cleaners, or visit the beauty parlor and have your hair washed and styled. Avoid planning weddings or ceremonies, and don't travel, but it is a good month in which to make appointments for the doctor, dentist, and podiatrist. Sports of all kinds will be enjoyable and lucky, so go swimming, go for a run, or take the children to the park for a game of soccer.
January 6 to February 3	
Chu—Discard	

Month 3

Month of the Tiger	This is a good time for major events, such as ceremonies, receptions, weddings, conferences, important meetings, and even moving to a new house. If you desire a cruise or some other kind of significant trip, that will be a good time to do it. Avoid small jobs and avoid cutting anything or planting things.
February 4 to March 5	
Man—Fullness	

Month 4

Month of the Rabbit	The time for major events is past, so finish things off, clear up, consider the outcome of the events, and recover from the recent activity. Don't start anything new yet, and even things that arise from these events can be left for a while. However, ancient lore said this was a good month for painting walls and doing good deeds, but a bad time for cutting, planting, or opening waterways.
March 6 to April 4	
Ping—Balance	

Month 5

Month of the Dragon April 5 to May 5 Ding—Arrange	Go back to work now, especially anything related to farming and animals. Plow the land, or prepare beds for planting, clear wells, and get going. Other kinds of work or business are also advised, but you need to keep your opinions to yourself and mind your own business.

Month 6

Month of the Snake May 6 to June 5 Zhi—Grasp	This is not a good time to go anywhere, so avoid traveling or doing anything away from your workplace or home. Travel is not the only problem as other things might also prove more expensive than you had planned.

Month 7

Month of the Horse June 6 to July 7 Po—Ruin	About the only people who will have a good month now are the police, who will be able to catch criminals easily. Otherwise, everything will be difficult, with conflict and disagreements all around. Keep away from people and keep your head down. Maybe go fishing, as that seems relatively safe.

Month 8	
Month of the Goat	Nothing much will happen this month, and the weather may be bad, so don't try to do anything other than pour yourself a nice drink and relax.
July 8 to August 7	
Wei—Danger	

Month 9	
Month of the Monkey	This is a lucky month for large-scale activity and long journeys that involve staying away from home for a while. Keep busy, do your work, and don't involve yourself in the affairs of others; in short, keep your opinions to yourself.
August 8 to September 7	
Cheng— Completion	

Month 10	
Month of the Rooster	This is a good time for anything to do with education, studying, and planning for the future. It's also a good month for trade and business, but not for travel, arranging funerals, going to the doctor or dentist, or other medical therapies.
September 8 to October 8	
Shou—Acceptance	

Month 11

Month of the Dog	This is a good month for those recovering from illness, surgery, and other medical issues; it is also an excellent time to communicate with people, generate business, do the bookkeeping, and write emails. This is a good time for short journeys, hobbies, and craftwork. It is a propitious phase for studying and training, but it is not a good period for heavy work, such as construction jobs.
October 9 to November 7	
Kai—Recovery	

Month 12

Month of the Pig	This is considered a difficult month and a poor time to start anything important, so the advice is to avoid as much stress as possible. It is a good idea now to get in touch with old friends, send invitations, advertise and market goods, or work on your social media. It is also said to be an excellent time to make resolutions and start a diet.
November 8— December 6	
Bi—Closed	

❈ ❈ ❈

9

THE DAY AND HOUR
SIGNS AND THE FOUR
PILLARS OF DESTINY

The Day Sign

The day sign provides information on yet another layer of our personality. It represents an aspect that is much less obvious than the year or month signs, since only those whom we love and trust see this side of our nature.

The ancient traditional calendar for finding a person's day sign, "The Ten Thousand Year Calendar," is huge and can be difficult to find in English. So the simplest way to determine your four pillars for the hour, day, month, and year of birth is to find an online calculator called "The Four Pillars of Destiny." There are plenty of these sites available; they are free of charge and easy to use. My current favorite is **psychicscience.org/pillars,** which is very easy to understand.

The Hour Sign

The hour sign is determined from the time of birth at the place of birth. Each of the twelve animal signs rules two hours of every day. Needless to say, this reveals another layer to one's personality, often a person's true needs and desires.

A good example of how the hour sign affects personality would be someone who appeared to be meek and mild on the outside but who has the ambitious Rat, fierce Tiger, stubborn Ox, or some other strong sign hidden away in the hour sign. Or alternatively, someone who appears strong and confident but who has the Goat or Pig as the hour sign, making these subjects real softies on the inside

Time Change Considerations

One thing you may have to take into account is Daylight Saving Time in the US or British Summer Time in the UK, as in these cases you need to deduct one hour from the birth time.

Times for the Hour Signs

Hour	Sign
11 p.m. to 1 a.m.	Rat
1 a.m. to 3 a.m.	Ox
3 a.m. to 5 a.m.	Tiger
5 a.m. to 7 a.m.	Rabbit
7 a.m. to 9 a.m.	Dragon
9 a.m. to 11 a.m.	Snake
11 a.m. to 1 p.m.	Horse
1 p.m. to 3 p.m.	Goat
3 p.m. to 5 p.m.	Monkey
5 p.m. to 7 p.m.	Rooster
7 p.m. to 9 p.m.	Dog
9 p.m. to 11 p.m.	Pig

The Four Pillars system is the astrological chart that shows the elements and animal signs that were in effect when a person was born. The system contains many layers of information, and it allows us to learn about fortunes at different times of life. The Four Pillars table looks something like the chart below, although it will probably include the Chinese names for the animal signs and the elements and other information. This is the type of information you will need:

Example of the Bazi or Four Pillars of Destiny Chart

Hour	Day	Month	Year
Wood	Earth	Fire	Metal
Tiger	Monkey	Rabbit	Pig

How to Read the Pillars or Columns

There are some crucial things to bear in mind when reading the chart:

THE TIMELINE

This shows what happens to us and influences us, and also the way we grow, develop, and behave at different times of our lives.

- **The year pillar** shows what happens to us and how we act during childhood and youth.
- **The month pillar** shows what happens to us and how we are during adulthood.
- **The day pillar** shows what happens to us and how we are during middle age.
- **The hour pillar** shows how we are during old age.

RELATIONSHIPS AND OTHER PEOPLE

This refers to the way we relate to others and also the way they relate to us. It may even refer to *their* personalities and behavior rather than *ours*.

- **The year pillar** refers to the family background and to our grandparents. Anything that happened to our families in the past and experiences that are passed down as family history or that we pick up from their behavior can influence us. Carl Jung called this the collective unconscious.
- **The month pillar** refers to parents and siblings, so it can demonstrate the way we get along with them, but it often demonstrates *their* natures and the way *they* behave rather than *our* natures and the way *we* behave.
- **The day pillar** shows our feelings about ourselves but also the way we relate to our lovers, and importantly, also the way our lovers relate to us. It can tell a lot about the nature of those whom we trust and with whom we are especially close.
- **The hour pillar** relates to our children and the way they turn out.

PERSONALITY

- **The year pillar** represents the outermost personality, partially due to the influences we received in childhood.
- **The month pillar** represents our outer manner, especially the way we operate as adults at work or in the wider world.
- **The day pillar** shows our inner manner and the way we are at home and in private.
- **The hour pillar** refers to our innermost nature, along with our hidden fears, hopes, and wishes.

The Year Pillar in Detail

AGE GROUP

If you are looking back over your own life or if you are checking out the life of a young person, this is the column you need to take into consideration, because it rules the ages from birth to eighteen.

The year pillar rules early influences, including parents, schoolteachers, friends, and the society in which we grow up. It shows how we were treated as children, and the amount of confidence we developed as a result of helpful influences around us, or whether we were so squashed during childhood that we never developed self-worth or the ability to stand up for ourselves. It shows the type of characteristics and skills that we developed when young and perhaps thought would become part of our future lives.

GENERAL DATA

This represents our *outer* manner and the *first impression* we give others. It also describes the surroundings and general lifestyle that we find ourselves living in, especially during our childhood and youth. It is probably a reflection of the behavior that others wanted from us when we were young and a result of the way we were treated when children.

This pillar is associated with the outside world and outsiders, so tradition says that these are people whose opinion about us is of no importance to us.

FAMILY AND CONNECTIONS

This rules our grandparents, ancestors, family background, and family history.

AT WORK

This links to those bosses, leaders, influential people, and possibly politicians with whom we rarely come into contact, but whose politics or preferences are those that we are bound to follow simply by working in that particular place.

The Month Pillar in Detail

AGE GROUP

The month pillar rules our lives from the ages of eighteen to thirty-four. This is the time when we develop our individuality, make strides in our profession, and learn from life. It is when we make important friendships and relationships, and it is when many of us bring children into the world. Our health is at its best, and we are still young enough to have fun and enjoy life.

This is the phase when we find our way in life and make headway in our careers. It is also the time when we are happy in our relationships and with our families or realize we have made a mistake and end our marriages and look for new partners.

GENERAL DATA

The month sign rules our general character and the part of our outer manner that is known to our acquaintances and people we are friendly with but not particularly close.

FAMILY AND CONNECTIONS

The month sign links with our relationship with our parents and the way we relate to our siblings. It can also refer to their behavior toward us.

AT WORK

This rules the superiors and bosses whom we deal with on a frequent basis and whom we get along with well enough.

The Day Pillar in Detail

AGE GROUP

This pillar rules the ages from thirty-five to fifty-one. This is a time when we leave childhood and youth behind and take responsibility for ourselves, and focus on our relationships and our careers, while bringing up our children and enjoying our friends and our social lives. This is when we become involved in the things that interest us, which may be sports, religious institutions, politics, special interest groups, or our friends.

We are at our most vigorous now, so we can forge ahead with our careers, use our skills and talents to the full, and lay the foundations for the wealth that we will obtain—and hopefully keep—during the rest of our lives.

GENERAL DATA

This pillar is said to relate to ourselves and to our health and well-being. This pillar represents our inner personality; we share our beliefs and feelings only with those whom we love and trust.

FAMILY AND CONNECTIONS

This sign concerns our own selves but also those with whom we have deep relationships, such as spouses, partners, lovers, or anyone about whom we have strong feelings. It shows the kind of people we connect with and the way they treat us.

AT WORK

This pillar rules those who help us, so this means mentors, helpful superiors, and those who take care of us, especially through difficult phases at our workplace.

The Hour Pillar in Detail
AGE GROUP
This relates to later life from the age of fifty-two upward. This is a time of reflection as we leave our youth behind with all that implies. It is a time when women go through menopause and when men feel less virile and vigorous than they once did. We should be at the height of our careers now, making our way at full speed and either happy with family life or making changes for the better.

GENERAL DATA
This sign represents the inner personality, our private thoughts, beliefs, and the secrets that we don't share with anybody else at all.

The hour sign is linked to creativity and to our hopes and dreams, which are private. This column truly represents what goes on inside our own heads.

FAMILY AND CONNECTIONS
This relates to our children and the way we feel about them. It can show how they turn out in the long run.

AT WORK
Where our jobs are concerned, this pillar relates to our colleagues and those with whom we get on well and who help and encourage us.

10

A FOUR PILLARS
CHART IN ACTION

To help understand how a person's sign can affect their life, I've provided an overview of internationally famous actress, dancer, and singer Kylie Minogue, who has sold a massive 80 million records.

Kylie Minogue

Data: Born on May 28, 1968, at 11 a.m. in Melbourne, Victoria, Australia, 37 degrees and 49 minutes south, 144 degrees and 58 minutes east.

Kylie comes from a Welsh/Irish background, with a father who was an accountant and a mother who had been a ballet dancer. Kylie's sister, Dannii, is a television personality and singer, and her brother is a news cameraman.

Kylie's family moved around a lot when she was young, which made her unsettled and unhappy, and she didn't make friends at school, so she spent her time learning to sing, dance, act, and play the violin and the piano. She and Dannii were encouraged to act professionally as children, but the experience of being shouted at by directors unnerved Kylie, and it took several years before she felt comfortable in that world. Her breakthrough came in 1986, when she landed the part of Charlene Robinson in the Melbourne soap opera *Neighbours*. Some years later, she decided to give her acting career a rest and focus on her singing—a decision that propelled her to international stardom.

Kylie likes to preserve her privacy; she has never married or had children. Kylie has become something of an icon in the gay community, and although she is not gay herself, she is delighted to have fans among that community.

Kylie was diagnosed with breast cancer in 2005 at the age of thirty-six and had treatment in Australia and France. Fortunately, she is now in remission. Interestingly, the age of thirty-six is an important one, because the annual animal system returns every twelve years, and these years are likely to be memorable for both good and bad reasons.

Hour	Day	Month	Year
Yang Earth	Yang Earth	Yin Fire	Yang Earth
Horse	Dog	Snake	Monkey

Kylie's Year Pillar
YANG EARTH MONKEY

Kylie's childhood and youth are characterized by her year pillar, which is the yang Earth Monkey. The parents of an Earth Monkey child are hardworking and upwardly mobile, and they pass their work ethic on to their children. The children don't do particularly well at school, but they succeed later, often in unusual or glamorous fields of work. Many members of this sign love music, and they enjoy active interests such as sports or dancing. The Monkey loves to read widely, and apparently Kylie has always loved reading. Despite the Earth Monkey's lack of obvious success during childhood, this is a proud combination that has great potential when it finds the right avenue. Earth Monkeys can overcome setbacks, take advantage of new opportunities, and reinvent themselves whenever a new start is needed.

Kylie's Month Pillar
YIN FIRE SNAKE

The Month Pillar rules our lives from the ages of eighteen to thirty-four, and it is when we make headway in our careers. It is also when we make good friends, link with colleagues and mentors, and get into personal relationships and start families. Kylie poured her energies into her work at this time and made important connections for her career. She left her parents and family in Australia while traveling around the world with her work. Snakes take their jobs very seriously, and they can overwork, while also trying to make the money that will provide a comfortable lifestyle for their parents and other family members. Snakes have a tendency to worry about financial or job security and to be uncertain as to whether the lucky streaks that come their way will keep going. The element of Fire makes them adventurous, somewhat impulsive, and competitive, but the yin aspect of Kylie's Fire element also makes her idealistic and generous, as we see from her philanthropic work in the field of cancer awareness for women.

Kylie's Day Pillar
YANG EARTH DOG

We start to head into middle age here, because the Day Pillar relates to the ages of thirty-five to fifty-one. The practical and ambitious Earth element is back in evidence here, along with the hardworking sign of the Dog, so it is likely that Kylie took on too much work during this time and stressed herself out. This period also marks the time when she became sick and needed a prolonged break from work. It's hard to believe this, but Kylie may have worried about money, and she may have been plagued with doubts as to whether her career would regenerate once she recovered from her treatment. The Dog is an idealistic sign that likes to help others, and it was during this phase that Kylie did much to promote awareness about cancer in women, and she has been honored by the Australian, British, and French governments for her humanitarian work.

Kylie's Hour Pillar
YANG EARTH HORSE

This Pillar leads on to older age, and it is clear that Kylie could afford to retire now, but it is likely that she will keep on working, albeit in a less demanding way than in the past. The ambitious yang Earth influence shows Kylie still has things she wants to achieve, while the restless Horse tells us that sitting still is not her style. Her internal nature shows that she is hardworking, devoted to her family, and fun to be with. She is bright and intelligent and well-read, with a wide range of knowledge about many different subjects. Kylie probably has homes in various different countries, because she would become bored if she stayed in one place for too long. Like the Horse that rules her inner nature, she needs to be on the move for work and for pleasure.

Kylie needs one or two trustworthy pals with whom she can talk over her problems, and she is also good at counseling others when they need sensible advice. The Horse is a strong sign, so her health should improve during this phase, but she must avoid working too hard or worrying too much. The Horse can be unpleasant when in a bad mood, so she must avoid giving her lover the silent treatment or being too critical. Such a big emphasis on Earth in her chart suggests obstinacy, and while a high level of determination is needed for a career of her magnitude, a stubborn attitude about things that don't really matter would get others down. Her chart suggests that Kylie should learn relaxation techniques and be a bit more easygoing for the sake of her own health and well-being.

CONCLUSION

I have had many books published over the years, but I can honestly say that Chinese astrology is the most complex subject I have ever tackled. I am known for making complex topics clear, and I hope I have achieved my objective this time around—but I am also aware that I have only scratched the surface of this enormous subject. Some of you will love the full Four Pillars chapters, but I suspect that for most readers, the basics will be enough, so for that reason, I have tried to make the sizable first part of this book as comprehensive and as engaging as possible.

I suggest that you keep this book on your shelf for reference, so you can check out the nature of your friends, loved ones, and even those people who puzzle you or upset you. Also, check out your own fortunes whenever you need some guidance.

One last note . . . if you are going through an unlucky phase, buy yourself a little piece of jade and keep it on your person. And wear something red, because the Chinese believe red is a lucky color!

I hope my love of all forms of astrology comes across to you and inspires you to take an interest in these fascinating subjects for yourself.

Good luck,
Sasha

✳ ✳ ✳

INDEX

BIBLIOGRAPHY

Aylward, Thomas F. *The Imperial Guide to Feng Shui & Chinese Astrology* (Watkins Publishing, 2007)

Augier, Serve. *Ba Zi: The Four Pillars of Destiny* (Singing Dragon, 2016)

Craze, Richard. *Practical Feng Shui: The Chinese Art of Living in Harmony with Your Surroundings* (Lorenz Books, 1997)

S.T., Althea. *A Course in Chinese Astrology: Reveal Your Destiny, Harness Your Luck with Four Pillars* (CreateSpace Publishing, 2017)

Thompson, Gerry Maguire. *The Guide to Chinese Horoscopes* (Watkins Publishing, 2012)

Walter, Derek. *Chinese Astrology: The Most Comprehensive Study of the Subject Ever Published in the English Language* (Watkins Publishing, 2005)

Yap, Joey. *The Power of X: Enter the 10 Gods* (Joey Yap Research Group, 2011)

ABOUT THE AUTHOR

After longing to know what made people tick, Sasha Fenton found astrology to give her the answers she was seeking. Sasha has written astrology columns for many magazines and newspapers and numerous books within the mind, body, and spirit subjects, including *In Focus Astrology* and *In Focus Numerology*. She has appeared on radio and television programs and presented talks and workshops at spiritual and astrological festivals around the world. She served as president of the British Astrological and Psychic Society, was former chair of the Advisory Panel on Astrological Education, and was a past member of the executive council of the Writers' Guild of Great Britain. Most recently, she helped launch MBS Professionals Ltd., a business-to-business service for those who work in the Mind, Body and Spirit professions. She lives in western England.

IMAGE CREDITS